DANIEL

STAND
on the
WORD
Study Guide

DANIEL

VISIONS
AND
VALOR

A 13-Day Journey through the Word
with Tony Perkins

FAMILY RESEARCH COUNCIL
SINCE 1983

FIDELIS PUBLISHING ®

ISBN: 9798992418651

Daniel: Visions and Valor
A Stand on the Word Study Guide

Content contributor: Dr. Kenyn Cureton
Cover design: Diana Lawrence
Interior layout design/typesetting: Lisa Parnell
Edited by: Lisa Guest

Order at www.faithfultext.com for a significant discount.
Email info@fidelispublishing.com to inquire about bulk purchase discounts.

Fidelis Publishing, LLC Sterling, VA • Nashville, TN
www.fidelispublishing.com

Manufactured in the United States of America

10 9 8 7 6 5 4 3 2 1

FIDELIS
PUBLISHING

Contents

— Day 1 —

Daniel: An Introduction

Welcome to the Stand on the Word Study Guide on Daniel! This book is the account of a prophetic man of God whose life was marked by purpose and by prayer. His advancement came through adversity and challenges that many would say were unfair, but God used those difficulties as opportunities as Daniel looked to and yielded to Him.

Now let's begin with some background on the book of Daniel. As we've talked about before, Daniel was a contemporary of Ezekiel and Jeremiah, but each had his designated lane of ministry that complemented the others. Daniel's name means "God is my judge." Daniel was taken captive by Nebuchadnezzar in the first deportation, which took place in 606 BC. His exact age is not known, but he was young. Various scholars place him between the ages of 12 and 17, and I'll comment on that aspect a little bit later. He came from the tribe of Judah and most likely from the royal family. He did not have the office of prophet or priest, although he was called a prophet by Jesus, and rightfully so. His book can be divided into two parts: historical and prophetic.

The first half of Daniel is mainly a historical account. His life in Babylon covered the entire span of the 70 years of captivity of the Jewish people from start to finish. Consequently, Daniel saw within his lifetime the rise and fall of the first great world empire. Daniel was there in Babylon when that city reached its zenith of power and splendor under Nebuchadnezzar, who was king. He reigned for 45 years. In all, Daniel eventually served under six rulers, and sometimes the regime change was the result of a hostile takeover. It wasn't like the relatively easy transitions we experience in America today.

Babylon is a key city in the Bible. It was situated in what many consider the cradle of civilization. In fact, some Bible scholars suggest it was near the place of the Garden of Eden. Today it is an uninhabited pile of ancient rubble. But in Daniel's day, Babylon was the premier city of the ancient Near East. It was the place of the Tower of Babel. It was home to Nebuchadnezzar's Hanging Gardens, one of the Seven Wonders of the Ancient World. Babylon under Nebuchadnezzar was a massive, fortified city. The walls were 300 feet high. They went into the ground some 25 feet, so an enemy couldn't tunnel underneath them. They were 80 feet thick, stretching 60 miles around the city.

Today, we sift through the ruins of this once great empire. It's a reminder of the fleeting nature of the things of this earth, even the most powerful things and those that appear as if they'll stand forever—something we need to remind ourselves of now. Also in the rubble is found evidence of the source of its weakness: its idolatry, its extravagance, and its wicked luxury, which historians and scholars say was unsurpassed in the history of the world. The city of Babylon was given to excess. That's why Babylon is a representative type. It's symbolic of the world. Yet despite its military and economic greatness, it's gone, and that's going to be the case for the world. But there is a Kingdom that is everlasting. It is the Kingdom of God. And you need to make sure you have your citizenship in the Kingdom of God. And that comes by trusting Jesus Christ as your Lord and Savior.

The second half of the book of Daniel is mainly prophetic, stretching from the days in which he lived all the way to the First and Second Coming of the Messiah. Now, in the prophetic portion of Daniel, in large part, this is what the critics have seized upon, claiming that Daniel could not have written the book, saying it had to have been written during the time of the Maccabees, which was 170 to 164 BC. That was after the events of Antiochus, whose actions Daniel's prophecies speak of in great detail. They say, "Well, it's just way too precise to have been written then. It had to have been written after the fact." But isn't that the nature of divine prophecy? Several sources point to the book of Daniel's existence, though, way before the Maccabean time, including Jewish historian Josephus, who provides in his writings the account of Alexander the Great coming to punish the Jewish people in 332 BC for their alliance to Darius. The high priest Jaddua met Alexander on his way to the city of Jerusalem and showed him a prophecy of Daniel, and it was the prophecy concerning Alexander. Alexander's wrath was then turned to favor, and he actually worshipped in the Jewish temple.

Now, the captivity of Daniel also marks a turning point in Israel's history and, really, the history of the world. This marks the beginning of the times of the Gentiles. The theocracy had ended. As A. R. Faussett wrote, "Earlier prophets from the standpoint of Israel treated Israel in its relationship to the world powers. Daniel from Babylon, the center of the then world power, treats the world powers in their relationship to Israel." So there's a shift in the focus. Faussett also pointed out that Daniel's residence in Babylon and his high official position there gave him an insight into world politics and the geopolitical scene, fitting him to be the recipient of political revelations.

Meanwhile, Daniel's spiritual experiences gained through Nebuchadnezzar's humiliation, Belshazzar's downfall, and the rapid decay of the Babylonian Empire itself, as well as the miraculous deliverances of himself and his friends, all fitted him for the ability to regard things from a spiritual standpoint. So he had this integrated understanding of the geopolitical along with the spiritual, which we will see in this book.

Daniel is a fascinating book. As we get into it, we'll talk more about the spiritual side of the political when it's revealed to him, and it's going to be captivating when we get to that. Again, welcome to this journey through the book of Daniel!

How to Get the Most from the Study Guide

While the study guide offers spiritual insights and applications, the real impact comes from the words of Scripture, which is the Word of God. Please read the selected text for the day in your own Bible. God's Word is "living and powerful" (Hebrews 4:12). The Spirit of God uses His Word to change your life. Nothing else can do that. So before reading the daily commentary, read God's Word!

In fact, here are five habits to cultivate as you approach God's Word each day:

1. ***Read it through:*** Don't skip around. Read the entire selection of Scripture. If you are pressed for time, please read

the Bible before you read the study guide notes. So read it through.

2. *Think it over:* Meditate on it. Let it marinate in your mind. If you can, take notes. We provide a notes page at the end of each day. Think it over.
3. *Pray it in:* Personalize the Scripture. Turn the verse that speaks to you into a prayer and then pray it into your life. Ask God what you need to do in response. This leads to the next habit.
4. *Live it out:* Consider ways to apply what God is revealing to you and ways you can obey Him. Put His Word into practice. Make it a part of who you are, how you think, how you speak, and how you behave toward God and other people. In other words, take God's Word and live it out.
5. *Pass it on.* Don't keep it to yourself. There are people in your life who need the same truth God has spoken to you in His Word. Share it. Pass it on.

About Stand on the Word

Stand on the Word is a ministry of Family Research Council, whose mission is to serve in the kingdom of God by championing faith, family, and freedom in public policy and in the culture from a biblical worldview. The purpose of Stand on the Word is to lay the foundation for a biblical worldview through daily reading and application of God's Word. For the daily journey, we have created a chronologically prioritized reading plan through the entire Bible that can be accessed at frc.org/Bible or simply by texting the word *Bible* to 67742.

Babylonian Empire

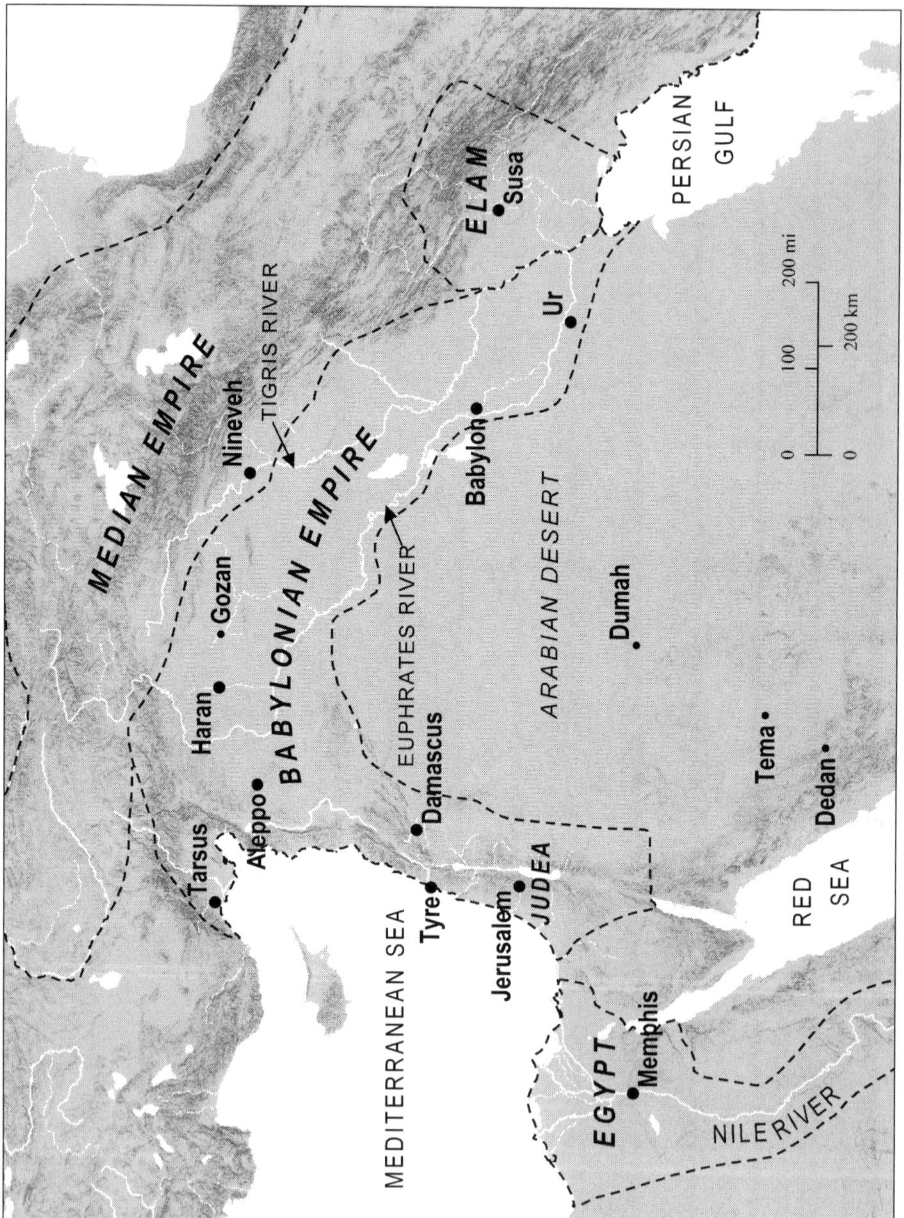

— Day 2 —

Today's Reading: Daniel 1

Verse of the Day

> "Now God had brought Daniel into the favor and goodwill of the chief of the eunuchs."
>
> — *Daniel 1:9*

Please read the entire Scripture selection in your own Bible and highlight or underline verses that stand out to you before you read the observations and engage the questions below.

Today we begin the remarkable book of Daniel. I want to direct your attention to Daniel 1:9: "Now God had brought Daniel into the favor and goodwill of the chief of the eunuchs." Nothing replaces the favor of God as we will see in this first chapter.

Let's go back and pick up with Daniel 1:1–2:

> In the third year of the reign of Jehoiakim king of Judah, Nebuchadnezzar king of Babylon came to Jerusalem and besieged it. And the Lord gave Jehoiakim king of Judah into his hand, with some of the articles of the house of God, which he carried into the land of Shinar to the house of his god; and he brought the articles into the treasure house of his god.

Now, make a note of these vessels. These were holy unto the Lord, and we're going to see them again in chapter 5. Profaning that which is holy to the Lord often becomes the instrument of our own downfall.

Let's continue in Daniel 1:3–4:

> Then the king instructed Ashpenaz, the master of his eunuchs, to bring some of the children of Israel and some of the king's descendants and some of the nobles, young men in whom there was no blemish, but good-looking, gifted in all wisdom, possessing knowledge and quick to understand, who had ability to serve in the king's palace, and whom they might teach the language and literature of the Chaldeans.

He probably gave them some kind of IQ test. That's why we know that there's a high probability that Daniel was from the royal family. Again, we don't know the exact age. But the clear implication that we see from this are young, pliable, moldable children that can be indoctrinated and trained in the ways of the Babylonians or the Chaldeans.

We are talking about a person's worldview here. According to the research of Christian sociologist and pollster George Barna, a worldview is formulated between the ages of 15 months and 13 years.[1] That explains the unrelenting effort of government to educate children at earlier and earlier ages. It is not a benevolent act of the government trying to help out parents. It is exactly what the Babylonians were doing in Daniel's day—indoctrination. Now, in the account of Daniel, we will see how children were inoculated against this indoctrination effort. And Daniel is an example of that.

Look at Daniel 1:5–8:

> The king appointed for them a daily provision of the king's delicacies and of the wine which he drank, and three years of training for them, so that at the end of that time they might serve before the king. Now from among those of the sons of Judah were Daniel, Hananiah, Mishael, and Azariah. To them the chief of the eunuchs gave names: he gave Daniel the name Belteshazzar; to Hananiah, Shadrach; to Mishael, Meshach; and to Azariah, Abed-Nego.
>
> But Daniel purposed in his heart that he would not defile himself with the portion of the king's delicacies, nor with the wine which he drank; therefore he requested of the chief of the eunuchs that he might not defile himself.

Now where did Daniel come up with that idea? I mean, it wasn't in the magazine rack on the back of the camel that he was walking behind on his way to captivity. It certainly wasn't some kind of Babylonian program that he picked this up from. We don't read this, but I think we can confidently assume that his parents taught him to follow the Lord as a child. His worldview was formulated by his parents.

Look back at our main verse, which is Daniel 1:9:

> Now God had brought Daniel into the favor and goodwill of the chief of the eunuchs.

Again, this is the key: the favor of God. Where does that come from? How do we get the favor of God? Well, we really can't earn it. God's favor is there. It's like His grace. But His favor is upon those who are obedient to Him, those who seek after Him. And you can't expect the favor of God if you reject the things of God. Now you may know the rest of this story. Daniel and his three friends excelled, and they were promoted (2:48–49). The final verse of chapter 1 is the bookend of the captivity, not Daniel's life. He lived a few years longer in captivity. Look at Daniel 1:21: "Thus Daniel continued until the first year of King Cyrus." So, that's chapter 1. Next time we're going to look at this question: "Will you stand?"

Questions for Reflection and Discussion

1. Why did the Babylonians give Daniel and his three friends new names that reflected the names of their gods (see v. 6)?
2. When Daniel remained obedient to the law of God by refusing to eat the king's nonkosher food, how did God bless him and his three friends (see vv. 8–20)?
   a. God gave Daniel favor and compassion with Ashpenaz, the man in charge.
   b. God gave them learning and skill in all literature and wisdom—ten times greater than the others.
   c. God gave Daniel understanding in all visions and dreams.
   d. All of the above

Notes on Today's Bible Reading

— Day 3 —

Today's Reading: Daniel 2

Verse of the Day

"He changes times and seasons;
he removes kings and sets up kings;
he gives wisdom to the wise
and knowledge to those who have understanding."

— Daniel 2:21

Please read the entire Scripture selection in your own Bible and highlight or underline verses that stand out to you before you read the observations and engage the questions below.

Today we are studying the second chapter of Daniel. I've entitled this devotional lesson "The Power of United Prayer." Beginning in this chapter, the book of Daniel contains biblical prophecy, which really provides the foundation for much of the biblical prophecy that is yet to be fulfilled.

In your Bible, especially if it is a study Bible, you'll probably have a notation that beginning in Daniel 2:4 through Daniel 7, the original language of the passage was Aramaic. That was the common language used throughout the Babylonian empire for diplomatic and commercial activity. What's the significance of that?

Well, this was not a message to the Jewish people who were in captivity. Remember, Ezekiel and Jeremiah were prophesying at the same time, primarily to the Jews. Daniel's message was primarily to the Gentile world about what was to come. It's very important to note that. We'll see in this chapter that this covers the four major world kingdoms and ends in the Second Coming of Jesus Christ and the establishment of His reign. But as we'll also see in this chapter, it is filled with very practical biblical truths that have application to our lives, which is why I've entitled this study "The Power of United Prayer." It's a very practical, applicable message for us today.

The application of Scripture is essential. Therefore, we should approach the historical and the prophetic portions of Scripture in the same manner that we would consider the Ten Commandments or the Sermon on the Mount. And that is by asking the question "What are the biblical truths and the principles that we read in these passages, and how should we apply them to our lives?" So, with that, let me provide some historical context.

There is some debate about when the events of Daniel 2 took place. Daniel 2:1 reads, "Now in the second year of Nebuchadnezzar's reign." But he co-reigned with his father and became king either in late 605 BC or in 604 BC. So most likely this took place in 602 BC, three years after Daniel and his friends had been carried away captive to Babylon.

Let's begin by looking at the dream and what really sets the stage for this entire chapter. Daniel 2:1–5 says:

> Now in the second year of Nebuchadnezzar's reign, Nebuchadnezzar had dreams; and his spirit was so troubled that his sleep left him. Then the king gave the command to call

> the magicians, the astrologers, the sorcerers, and the Chaldeans to tell the king his dreams. So they came and stood before the king. And the king said to them, "I have had a dream, and my spirit is anxious to know the dream."
>
> Then the Chaldeans spoke to the king in Aramaic, "O king, live forever! Tell your servants the dream, and we will give the interpretation." The king answered and said to the Chaldeans, "My decision is firm: if you do not make known the dream to me, and its interpretation, you shall be cut in pieces, and your houses shall be made an ash heap."

In summary, the king had a dream, and the magicians said, "All right, tell us your dream, and we'll tell you the meaning." But he responded, "No, you tell me the dream *and* the interpretation." He wanted to make sure that these people knew what they were talking about. I'm going to talk more about this in our next session, but in reading this, we begin to detect that Nebuchadnezzar was suffering from some form of psychosis because he had these wild mood swings, going from one extreme to another. We see this throughout the book of Daniel. No interpretation was provided, and Nebuchadnezzar ordered the wise men to be executed as a result.

Let's continue in Daniel 2:13, "So the decree went out, and they began killing the wise men; and they sought Daniel and his companions, to kill them." So even though they were young, they had been in training to be wise men to serve the king. He was so angry he wanted to kill them all. Look at Daniel 2:14–18:

> Then with counsel and wisdom Daniel answered Arioch, the captain of the king's guard, who had gone out to kill the wise men of Babylon; he answered and said to Arioch the

> king's captain, "Why is the decree from the king so urgent?" Then Arioch made the decision known to Daniel.
>
> So Daniel went in and asked the king to give him time, that he might tell the king the interpretation. Then Daniel went to his house, and made the decision known to Hananiah, Mishael, and Azariah, his companions, that they might seek mercies from the God of heaven concerning this secret, so that Daniel and his companions might not perish with the rest of the wise men of Babylon.

I could spend a week on this one chapter because there are so many applicable truths within this prophetic chapter but let me just provide a few.

First, our lives are not without problems and challenges. Daniel, Hananiah, Mishael, and Azariah were all faithful to God in a godless culture, yet we see over and over in this book that they repeatedly faced challenges to their faith and to their lives. Being a follower of Jesus does not spare us from trouble. In fact, Jesus warned His disciples of what was to come in John 16:33, "These things I have spoken to you, that in Me you may have peace. In the world you will have tribulation; but be of good cheer, I have overcome the world." As we've seen in the lives of men throughout our journey through the Bible, it's not a one-and-done situation. It's not like we face difficulty, and it's smooth sailing from there. Standing for the truth of Scripture and advancing the Kingdom of God is a journey. And if we are to be successful in that journey, we must walk in the power and the peace of the Lord Jesus Christ that He spoke of. The question is, how do we do that? We do it through prayer.

Look at the power of uniting in prayer with other believers. With death at their door, these four men appealed to God for the revelation that no man could provide. And look what happened in Daniel 2:19, "Then the secret was revealed to Daniel in a night vision. So Daniel blessed the God of heaven." How did they respond? Immediately, even before delivering the dream and its interpretation to Nebuchadnezzar, they praised God. We must cultivate hearts of gratitude even in the midst of difficulty. Right now in America, in this godless culture where we have people in government that are hostile to faith and pushing evil and godless policies, we need to cultivate a heart of gratitude because out of that gratitude comes praise to our Lord and Savior Jesus Christ, wherein lies our power.

In Romans 1:18–32, ungodly people denied God and His authority as the Creator, and they had ungrateful hearts. When we fail to be thankful, that is a telltale sign of pending implosion. So let's cultivate hearts of gratitude and praise God. Look at Daniel 2:20–22:

Daniel answered and said:

> "Blessed be the name of God forever and ever,
> For wisdom and might are His.
> And He changes the times and the seasons;
> He removes kings and raises up kings;
> He gives wisdom to the wise
> And knowledge to those who have understanding.
> He reveals deep and secret things;
> He knows what is in the darkness,
> And light dwells with Him."

God knows all things. Nothing is hidden from God. And He shares these things with His people. The problem is that we don't spend time with Him listening to what He has to say.

If we want to know what's happening in the world around us and how we are to respond, we need to spend time in God's Word and in prayer. We spend that time in prayer, and we spend time in God's Word. That's how God speaks to us. Until we have exhausted His Word, we cannot expect to hear anything else from Him.

There are so many Christians today chasing a word. They need to read *the* Word of God. Look at Daniel 2:23:

> "I thank You and praise You,
> O God of my fathers;
> You have given me wisdom and might,
> And have now made known to me what we asked of You,
> For You have made known to us the king's demand."

Here is a dream and its prophetic meaning in Daniel 2:32–35:

> This image's head was of fine gold, its chest and arms of silver, its belly and thighs of bronze, its legs of iron, its feet partly of iron and partly of clay. You watched while a stone was cut out without hands, which struck the image on its feet of iron and clay, and broke them in pieces. Then the iron, the clay, the bronze, the silver, and the gold were crushed together, and became like chaff from the summer threshing floors; the wind carried them away so that no trace of them was found. And the stone that struck the image became a great mountain and filled the whole earth.

Beginning with the head, there was gold. Then the value and the content of the material decreased from there down to a mixture of clay and iron in the feet. Biblical scholars provide the interpretation of the description Daniel gave here. According to them, the head of gold was the Chaldean monarchy that, as we read in Jeremiah, would last 70 years. And that's what happened. This was the premier world empire, the first one of its kind, that would be replaced by the breast and two arms of silver, representing the Medes and the Persians. The Medes and Persians would then be superseded by the belly and thighs of brass, representing the Grecian monarchy founded by Alexander.

Finally, the legs and feet of iron represented the Roman monarchy and empire, which ended in ten kingdoms represented by the ten toes. We have then the stone that is not cut by human hands that smashes to powder all the rest. The stone is Jesus, and it represents the Kingdom of God. Matthew 21:44 says, "Whoever falls on this stone will be broken; but on whomever it falls, it will grind him to powder." Either we can come to Christ to be broken, to fall upon Him, and to receive His grace and mercy, or that stone will fall and crush whoever it falls upon.

Here's one final thought: this revelation is being and will be fulfilled. Take note: the Kingdom of God will prevail over the kingdoms of this world. This is why we can have confidence that the church—not the organized church in terms of denominations, but followers of Jesus Christ—is not going away. Don't pay any attention to the headlines implying that the church is declining, that Christians are going away, or that the Kingdom of God will not prevail. The gates of hell, the cancel culture, Hollywood, and the media will not prevail against the Kingdom of God. And if you're a follower of Jesus Christ, if you've accepted Him as your Lord and Savior, you are a citizen of the Kingdom of God. And as we read here in this prophetic word in Daniel, that Kingdom of God will prevail.

Questions for Reflection and Discussion

1. What did Daniel ask his three Hebrew friends to do when faced with the difficulty of giving an interpretation to King Nebuchadnezzar's dream under threat of death (see vv. 17–18)?
   a. Run for their lives.
   b. Prepare to defend themselves.
   c. Seek mercy from God.
   d. None of the above

2. What does the Bible say about God's relationship with rulers (see v. 21)?

Notes on Today's Bible Reading

— Day 4 —

Today's Reading: Daniel 3

Verse of the Day

> "Shadrach, Meshach, and Abed-Nego answered and said to the king, 'O Nebuchadnezzar, we have no need to answer you in this matter. If this be so, our God whom we serve is able to deliver us from the burning fiery furnace, and He will deliver us out of your hand, O king.'"
>
> — *Daniel 3:16–17*

Please read the entire Scripture selection in your own Bible and highlight or underline verses that stand out to you before you read the observations and engage the questions below.

Today we're going to dive into one of the most well-known accounts of a test of faith that we find in the Bible. Let's start with Daniel 3:16–17:

> Shadrach, Meshach, and Abed-Nego answered and said to the king, "O Nebuchadnezzar, we have no need to answer you in this matter. If that is the case, our God whom we serve is able to deliver us from the burning fiery furnace, and He will deliver us from your hand, O king."

Now, what child who attended Sunday School or Vacation Bible School during their childhood did not hear this story of the three Hebrews in the fiery furnace? But here's the problem: because this is so closely aligned with children's Bible stories, we're apt to kind of skim through the story or even limit its applicability to us. Remember the old flannelgraph stories? We just kind of think of it as it's a kids' story, but it's a real account of what happened to men who stood firm in their conviction. Now, let me just go back really quick. All the Bible is relevant, but I think this passage is extremely relevant to the times in which we are living now. We will again see the theme that I mentioned last time, and that is that advancement comes through adversity.

Here's the context of this chapter. The three young men who in the previous chapter were promoted by Nebuchadnezzar to leadership positions for their role in the revelation of his prophetic dream were summoned along with all the other leaders of the expansive kingdom of Nebuchadnezzar. So, this was essentially the whole known world, a large portion of which he had control over, that was called to the plain to witness what was about to take place. Now, the timing of this is not certain. There's some debate over it. The Septuagint says that it occurred in the eighteenth year of Nebuchadnezzar's reign, but other sources state that it was earlier. What we do know for certain is that he built this 90-foot golden statue. Now, as we read it, it'll sound very familiar. Some speculate it was actually a statue of Nebuchadnezzar, the head of gold from the earlier dream that Daniel interpreted.

Let's begin in Daniel 3:1–6:

> Nebuchadnezzar the king made an image of gold, whose height was sixty cubits and its width six cubits. He set it up

> in the plain of Dura, in the province of Babylon. And King Nebuchadnezzar sent word to gather together the satraps, the administrators, the governors, the counselors, the treasurers, the judges, the magistrates, and all the officials of the provinces, to come to the dedication of the image which King Nebuchadnezzar had set up. So the satraps, the administrators, the governors, the counselors, the treasurers, the judges, the magistrates, and all the officials of the provinces gathered together for the dedication of the image that King Nebuchadnezzar had set up; and they stood before the image that Nebuchadnezzar had set up. Then a herald cried aloud: "To you it is commanded, O peoples, nations, and languages, that at the time you hear the sound of the horn, flute, harp, lyre, and psaltery, in symphony with all kinds of music, you shall fall down and worship the gold image that King Nebuchadnezzar has set up; and whoever does not fall down and worship shall be cast immediately into the midst of a burning fiery furnace."

The pressure was already there, and you would think, based on this, that Nebuchadnezzar knew there was going to be some resistance. So he had a plan ready and was going to make an example of anyone who refused to bow down to this idol—which, as I pointed out, some suggest was a representation of him.

Let's continue in Daniel 3:7: "So at that time, when all the people heard the sound of the horn, flute, harp, and lyre, in symphony with all kinds of music, all the people, nations, and languages fell down and worshiped the gold image which King Nebuchadnezzar had set up." So they willingly complied. And that's usually where the majority of people are. But then we have Shadrach,

Meshach, and Abed-Nego. They refused to bow. And the Chaldeans, the so-called wise men who were exposed as frauds earlier by Daniel, were very quick to rat them out, not only for not bowing down on this occasion, but they went further in verse 12 to call them out for not serving the gods of Nebuchadnezzar.

Where was Daniel? He wasn't there. It's not recorded. Any suggestion that he was there is simply speculation. He could have been away on the king's business, or the king could have granted him leave. Frankly, we just don't know. But some scholars see his absence from this account as a prophetic portrayal of the tribulation. Daniel represents the church/body of Christ which is absent during the Great Tribulation when the judgment of God is poured out. I'm not going to delve into that aspect of this chapter, so let's focus on the principles that are clearly revealed in this remarkable chapter that I believe have tremendous application to our lives today.

Let's continue in Daniel 3:13, "Then Nebuchadnezzar, in rage and fury, gave the command to bring Shadrach, Meshach, and Abed-Nego. So they brought these men before the king." Now, another note: we've seen this behavior before in Nebuchadnezzar. He appeared to be mentally unstable. Or perhaps these fits of rage were a byproduct of pride, but nonetheless, we see him going from promoting these men in the previous chapter to prosecuting them. And again, we don't know exactly how much time had passed, but he certainly knew them. He went from promoting them and praising their God (he said this in Daniel 2:47: "Truly your God is the God of gods, the Lord of kings, and a revealer of secrets, since you could reveal this secret") to actually heating up the fiery furnace seven times hotter to dispatch these faithful servants to eternity. It's not that they had done anything else wrong. They just did not conform to this latest craze of the king. They did not conform to worshiping his idol.

Now, take note of this. In this passage, we see Nebuchadnezzar as a type of human government that vacillates from one extreme to another. Consider our own country over the last 30 to 40 years and the extreme shifts from one administration to another. I mean, it's almost like we have a bipolar government. One administration honors and protects the Christian faith and the faith of others, while the next will marginalize and even prosecute and persecute Christian beliefs. We have seen the government using its power and authority to force acceptance of that which people know is not real or not right. In other words, we see the same thing that happened in Daniel's day. What Nebuchadnezzar was doing, we see our own government doing today. It might not be politically correct to say that, but it's an accurate statement.

Look at Daniel 3:14–17:

> Nebuchadnezzar spoke, saying to them, "Is it true, Shadrach, Meshach, and Abed-Nego, that you do not serve my gods or worship the gold image which I have set up? Now if you are ready at the time you hear the sound of the horn, flute, harp, lyre, and psaltery, in symphony with all kinds of music, and you fall down and worship the image which I have made, good! But if you do not worship, you shall be cast immediately into the midst of a burning fiery furnace. And who is the god who will deliver you from my hands?"
>
> Shadrach, Meshach, and Abed-Nego answered and said to the king, "O Nebuchadnezzar, we have no need to answer you in this matter. If that is the case, our God whom

> we serve is able to deliver us from the burning fiery furnace, and He will deliver us from your hand, O king."

These courageous young men had confidence that God would help them whether it was delivering them from the fire or through the fire. They knew God was faithful. Look at what it says in Daniel 3:18, "But if not, let it be known to you, O king, that we do not serve your gods, nor will we worship the gold image which you have set up." Regardless of whether or not God delivers us, whether or not we see His hand immediately intervening, it does not matter. Our confidence is in God, and we know what He's called us to do, and we will not compromise. Now, I'm not going to delve into this now, but here is another side note. Consider the role music played in this mass deception. It's repeated over and over. We need to be aware of how music is often used to communicate and reinforce an ideology.

Nebuchadnezzar made an example of these men in front of these representatives. This is what he was doing. This is why the furnace was there. He wanted to make an example out of them in front of all these representatives from every geographical and political area of his kingdom, so that fear would spread in their hearts, which they would carry back to their respective homelands. That's what this was about. But God was about to show the known world His power and authority through His faithful servants. So here is where Nebuchadnezzar really messed up. Nebuchadnezzar made this not about these three young men, but about God. Look what he said in Daniel 3:15, "Who is the god who will deliver you from my hands?"

You see, this is actually where we need to be. We don't want to make it about us, but rather about the glory and the reputation of God, the One whom we serve. You want to see God move? Well, watch what happened when the oppressors challenged God's power and God's authority. In fact, when we pray, when we appeal to God, it is to His reputation and His name that we should be appealing for His intervention in the policies that now govern our own nation, which are not derived from the truth of heaven above. Quite frankly, they come from the deception of the pit of hell below, and I don't hesitate to say that. It is true.

How do these young men respond? In verse 16 they said, "O Nebuchadnezzar, we have no need to answer you in this matter." Their minds were made up. I think their decision was made back when they were first carried away captive along with Daniel, when they purposed in their hearts that they would not defile themselves with the delicacies offered to the idols that the king provided.

You see, the big day of testing that everyone sees here on that big global stage, if you will, is preceded by small choices of the heart that very few, if any, ever observe. That's your day of testing, before that great cloud of witnesses, and the big test will be preceded by these small decisions that we make to be faithful to God when no one else is watching.

Look at Daniel 3:17 again, "If that is the case, our God whom we serve is able to deliver us from the burning fiery furnace, and He will deliver us from your hand, O king." The bottom line is that God will deliver us *from* death or *through* death. Therefore, we will not conform. We will stand. It reminds me of Martin Luther, the man God used to spark the Protestant Reformation. He was on trial in 1521, over 500 years ago, at the Diet of Worms, and he was told to recant his writings that were critical of the pope and the lies and deception that covered the church. Luther said this, "I am conquered by the Holy Scriptures quoted by me, and my conscience is bound in the word of God: I can not and will not recant any thing, since it is unsafe and dangerous to do any thing against the conscience..." And then, although there's some debate about this, according to tradition, he said, "Here I stand, I can not do otherwise. So help me God. Amen![2]

You know the rest of the story of the three Hebrew young men. They were delivered, and the king was again moved to confess the greatness of the one true God. God's power is seen in the preservation of His faithful followers through the fiery trials of oppression. And standing in the face of oppression may be the spark that ignites repentance in the very heart of the oppressors. This is a tremendous example of faith and commitment to the Lord. All His Word is relevant to us. But this is a motivational word for us today in this country and in this culture in which we're living. We should strive to have the same faith of these three young men so that we will stand firm knowing that God will either deliver us out of the fire or through the fire.

So, here's a question for you today: Will you stand in the day when government officials force many to bow down to lies and deception? Will you face the fiery furnace of opposition and oppression? Will you do so in the confidence that your God will deliver you, and His name will be glorified?

Questions for Reflection and Discussion

1. Daniel's friends refused to bow down and worship King Nebuchadnezzar's pagan golden idol. When the king demanded to know why, what was their response (see vv. 16–18)?
   a. We don't need to answer you.
   b. Our God is able to deliver us.
   c. Even if He does not deliver us, we will not worship your idol.
   d. All of the above

2. Before God miraculously rescued the three Hebrews from the fiery furnace, what did the king see in the flames with them that astonished him (vv. 24–25)?

Notes on Today's Bible Reading

— Day 5 —

Today's Reading: Daniel 4

Verse of the Day

"This decision is by the decree of the watchers,
And the sentence by the word of the holy ones,
In order that the living may know
That the Most High rules the kingdom of men,
Gives it to whomever He will
And sets over it the lowest of men."

— Daniel 4:17

Please read the entire Scripture selection in your own Bible and highlight or underline verses that stand out to you before you read the observations and engage the questions below.

Today we are in Daniel 4, and our topic is when leaders go crazy. Our key verse is Daniel 4:17:

This decision is by the decree of the watchers,
And the sentence by the word of the holy ones,
In order that the living may know
That the Most High rules the kingdom of men,
Gives it to whomever He will
And sets over it the lowest of men.

This is another prophetic vision which is given to Nebuchadnezzar. This vision concerns the humbling that was going to be coming upon him because of his pride. I think every leader should read this chapter and focus in particular on verse 17. I'm going to talk a little bit more about that in a moment, but first the timeline for the events in this chapter, as we can best determine, are as follows. The dream came around the 34th or 35th year of Nebuchadnezzar's reign, which would have been about 572 BC. A year later, the prophetic dream was fulfilled when he refused to heed the advice that Daniel gave him. Nebuchadnezzar spent seven years in the wild, out of his mind. After that, he came to his senses and gave glory that is due to the one true God, and he returned to the throne for two years before he died at the age of 72.

Let's start in Daniel 4:1–3:

> Nebuchadnezzar the king,
> To all peoples, nations, and languages that dwell in all the earth:
> Peace be multiplied to you.
> I thought it good to declare the signs and wonders that the
> Most High God has worked for me.
> How great are His signs,
> And how mighty His wonders!
> His kingdom is an everlasting kingdom,
> And His dominion is from generation to generation.

Nebuchadnezzar is an enlightened man! This chapter begins with a prologue that is the conclusion of the ordeal that Nebuchadnezzar gave in detail. He recognized that there is only one King, and there is only one Kingdom that is all powerful and everlasting, and it is the one of the Most High God. Look at Daniel 4:4–5: "I,

Nebuchadnezzar, was at rest in my house, and flourishing in my palace. I saw a dream which made me afraid, and the thoughts on my bed and the visions of my head troubled me."

Now, he had the dream, and he again called upon the magicians, the astrologers, the Chaldeans, and the soothsayers to come to give him the interpretation. It was déjà vu all over again. Haven't we seen this before? Now, it had been a number of years, but there is no explanation given as to why he went back to the same people who couldn't help him with the previous vision and dream that he'd had years ago. So, out of options, he turned once again to Daniel. And we do know that there was a relationship between Daniel and him, so it seems a bit odd that he turned to Daniel last, but that's what the passage says.

Daniel reluctantly provided the interpretation because Nebuchadnezzar was his friend, and the interpretation was not good. Daniel was not excited about this word. Remember, Daniel was a captive serving in the Babylonian administration, yet he had favor from them and prayed for Nebuchadnezzar. Look at Daniel 4:19–22:

> Then Daniel, whose name was Belteshazzar, was astonished for a time, and his thoughts troubled him. So the king spoke, and said, "Belteshazzar, do not let the dream or its interpretation trouble you."
>
> Belteshazzar answered and said, "My lord, may the dream concern those who hate you, and its interpretation concern your enemies!
>
> "The tree that you saw, which grew and became strong, whose height reached to the heavens and which could be seen by all the earth, whose leaves were lovely and its

> fruit abundant, in which was food for all, under which the beasts of the field dwelt, and in whose branches the birds of the heaven had their home—it is you, O king, who have grown and become strong; for your greatness has grown and reaches to the heavens, and your dominion to the end of the earth."

Obviously, the great tree is symbolic of King Nebuchadnezzar. Let's continue in Daniel 4:23–27:

> "And inasmuch as the king saw a watcher, a holy one, coming down from heaven and saying, 'Chop down the tree and destroy it, but leave its stump and roots in the earth, bound with a band of iron and bronze in the tender grass of the field; let it be wet with the dew of heaven, and let him graze with the beasts of the field, till seven times pass over him'; this is the interpretation, O king, and this is the decree of the Most High, which has come upon my lord the king: They shall drive you from men, your dwelling shall be with the beasts of the field, and they shall make you eat grass like oxen. They shall wet you with the dew of heaven, and seven times shall pass over you, till you know that the Most High rules in the kingdom of men, and gives it to whomever He chooses.
>
> "And inasmuch as they gave the command to leave the stump and roots of the tree, your kingdom shall be assured to you, after you come to know that Heaven rules. Therefore, O king, let my advice be acceptable to you; break off your sins by being righteous, and your iniquities by showing

mercy to the poor. Perhaps there may be a lengthening of your prosperity."

Fragments of Babylonian cuneiform text support this biblical account as they describe the strange behavior of Nebuchadnezzar and his being separated from his family for a while. In that age, no one ever wrote anything negative about the king or the leadership. It was never recorded. So, it's not surprising that we do *not* see this. Yet this episode is instructive. We're going to see it through the rest of this journey. It's the presence and the problem of pride. It was pride: the refusal to recognize the sovereignty of God and that the Lord is above all people and all things led Nebuchadnezzar to this situation. This is why I said every leader should read this chapter and in particular focus on verse 17. Now let's look at Daniel 4:17 again:

"This decision is by the decree of the watchers,
And the sentence by the word of the holy ones,
In order that the living may know
That the Most High rules the kingdom of men,
Gives it to whomever He will
And sets over it the lowest of men."

The message is clear: God is God over all. He rules in the affairs of men.

Now, in our previous lessons on Daniel, I've referenced Nebuchadnezzar's mood swings or what we would describe as mental and emotional instability. Many scholars actually point to mental illness or psychosis in Nebuchadnezzar. Nebuchadnezzar would not be alone in this category among leaders. The list of rulers and leaders throughout history who have suffered some form of mental illness and instability is longer than we might think. Alexander the Great, Julius Caesar, Napoleon Bonaparte, King George the Third, Adolf Hitler, Joseph Stalin—and the list goes on. This doesn't even include some of the great writers and artists that also fell into this category.

Look again at the end of verse 17, "…In order that the living may know that the Most High rules the kingdom of men, gives it to whomever He will and sets over it the lowest of men." You see, God will not have rivals. Notice the words that Nebuchadnezzar spoke: "Look what I have done." When we take credit for what God has done, as Nebuchadnezzar did, we're in serious trouble. God will not have rivals. And pride is the door through which many of man's vexations walk. Proverbs 16:18 says, "Pride goes before destruction, / And a haughty spirit before a fall." When you see pride, when you see a haughty spirit, you know trouble is coming, and we should work and pray and be open to the Holy Spirit showing us those things in our own lives before it brings a fall.

Now look at the remedy or the preventative measures that Daniel gave to the king to ward off the pending judgment in Daniel 4:27, "Therefore, O king, let my advice be acceptable to you; break off your sins by being righteous, and your iniquities by showing mercy to the poor. Perhaps there may be a lengthening of your prosperity." Now read about the turning point for Nebuchadnezzar in Daniel 4:34–35:

> And at the end of the time I, Nebuchadnezzar, lifted my eyes to heaven, and my understanding returned to me; and I

blessed the Most High and praised and honored Him who lives forever:

> For His dominion is an everlasting dominion,
> And His kingdom is from generation to generation.
> All the inhabitants of the earth are reputed as nothing;
> He does according to His will in the army of heaven
> And among the inhabitants of the earth.
> No one can restrain His hand
> Or say to Him, "What have You done?"

This is a remarkable and instructive passage when you consider that Nebuchadnezzar ruled the first great world empire, and as we've seen, with each successive empire there was a devolution, a diminishing of their power and their authority and their reach. This was at the pinnacle. And after all of that he came at the very end to realize there is only one God, there is only one Supreme Ruler, and it wasn't him. It was the one true God. Nebuchadnezzar's eyes were open to the truth.

Questions for Reflection and Discussion

1. What was to happen to King Nebuchadnezzar as a result of his second dream (vv. 24–27)?
   a. Lose his mind
   b. Live with the beasts and eat grass like an ox
   c. Languish in his insane state for seven years
   d. All of the above

2. Humbled by the experience, what conclusion did the king make about God (vv. 34–37)?

Notes on Today's Bible Reading

— Day 6 —

Today's Reading: Daniel 5

Verse of the Day

> I have heard of you, that the Spirit of God is in you, and that light and understanding and excellent wisdom are found in you.
>
> — *Daniel 5:14*

Please read the entire Scripture selection in your own Bible and highlight or underline verses that stand out to you before you read the observations and engage the questions below.

Today we're in Daniel 5. Our topic is "The handwriting on the wall solving the perplexing problems of our day." Our key verse is Daniel 5:14 which says, "I have heard of you, that the Spirit of God is in you, and that light and understanding and excellent wisdom are found in you." Now in this chapter, Belshazzar, the grandson of Nebuchadnezzar, was king. And as history often reveals, if the lessons learned by the fathers are not intentionally taught and passed along to their children, those subsequent generations become lost. They drift.

At this point, roughly two decades had passed since Nebuchadnezzar had his experience where he declared praise and honored the King of heaven after God had humbled him as he spent seven years out at pasture. But now some 20 years later, Babylon was under siege by King Cyrus of Persia for two years. Belshazzar was confident because of Babylon's great defenses. They had an abundance of food in the city, 20 years' worth of provisions. They had water from the river Euphrates that ran through the middle of the city. So they were confident they could survive, and they continued in their drunken debauchery. But they didn't last 20 years. They only lasted two.

Let's start in Daniel 5:1–2:

> Belshazzar the king made a great feast for a thousand of his lords, and drank wine in the presence of the thousand. While he tasted the wine, Belshazzar gave the command to bring the gold and silver vessels which his father Nebuchadnezzar had taken from the temple which had been in Jerusalem, that the king and his lords, his wives, and his concubines might drink from them.

Now, you often see in Scripture where it says, "the father," but that can mean grandfather or great-grandfather. In this case it is his grandfather. Look at Daniel 5:3–4:

> Then they brought the gold vessels that had been taken from the temple of the house of God which had been in Jerusalem; and the king and his lords, his wives, and his concubines drank from them. They drank wine, and praised the gods of gold and silver, bronze and iron, wood and stone.

Here's the picture. Belshazzar had squared off with Cyrus in a battle two years previously. Cyrus routed him, so Belshazzar retreated back behind the walls of Babylon. So what did he do then?

Well, he arrogantly continued what had become a defining characteristic of Babylon, drunken debauchery. Remember the sacred vessels from the temple? We read about those over in chapter 1. Here they are. In his drunken arrogance, he called for them to be brought from the place where they had been safely kept for decades. Take note of this: defiling the sacred, taking the things of God lightly, having no fear or reverence for God was a red line for God.

Look at Daniel 5:5–6:

> In the same hour the fingers of a man's hand appeared and wrote opposite the lampstand on the plaster of the wall of the king's palace; and the king saw the part of the hand that wrote. Then the king's countenance changed, and his thoughts troubled him, so that the joints of his hips were loosened and his knees knocked against each other.

See, God can get our attention. To borrow a line from Elvis Presley, Belshazzar was "all shook up." Let's continue in Daniel 5:7:

> The king cried aloud to bring in the astrologers, the Chaldeans, and the soothsayers. The king spoke, saying to the wise men of Babylon, "Whoever reads this writing, and tells me its interpretation, shall be clothed with purple and have a chain of gold around his neck; and he shall be the third ruler in the kingdom."

Now many scholars believe the reason that whoever did this was to become the third ruler in the kingdom because there was actually a power sharing, a co-regency here between Belshazzar and his father.

Look at Daniel 5:8–9, "Now all the king's wise men came, but they could not read the writing, or make known to the king its interpretation. Then King Belshazzar was greatly troubled, his countenance was changed, and his lords were astonished." Here's something to take note of: those men and those nations who will not fear and reverence God will at some point be brought to a place where they are frightened by God.

Let's continue with Daniel 5:10–12

> The queen, because of the words of the king and his lords, came to the banquet hall. The queen spoke, saying, "O king, live forever! Do not let your thoughts trouble you, nor let your countenance change. There is a man in your kingdom in whom is the Spirit of the Holy God. And in the days of your father, light and understanding and wisdom, like the wisdom of the gods, were found in him; and King Nebuchadnezzar your father—your father the king—made him chief of the magicians, astrologers, Chaldeans, and soothsayers. Inasmuch as an excellent spirit, knowledge, understanding, interpreting dreams, solving riddles, and explaining enigmas were found in this Daniel, whom the king named Belteshazzar, now let Daniel be called, and he will give the interpretation."

As I mentioned earlier, Nebuchadnezzar would have been Belshazzar's grandfather and the queen was Belshazzar's mother. She was not at the party he was throwing, but apparently was summoned when he couldn't solve the problem of the handwriting on the wall. She came and told him of Daniel, who apparently had not been active in Belshazzar's administration.

Let's look at Daniel 5:13, "Then Daniel was brought in before the king. The king spoke, and said to Daniel, 'Are you that Daniel who is one of the captives from Judah, whom my father the king brought from Judah?'" Daniel was nearing 70 years old at this point, but notice here that he was still positioned and prepared to serve. He still was following God, and he was ready to serve.

I don't know if you've heard of the Heimlich maneuver, a very popular life-saving maneuver that was developed in the 1970s by Doctor Henry Heimlich. Now, it's not possible to calculate the number of lives that have been saved by this technique that is used when someone is choking. But it's clearly in the tens of thousands. Doctor Heimlich died of complications of a heart attack in 2016 at the age of 96. Before he died, he was living in a retirement community in Cincinnati, Ohio. Seven months prior to his death, he used the Heimlich maneuver to save the life of a woman who was also living in that retirement community. But it was the first time he had ever used the technique. He had designed it, pioneered it, and helped other people use it. But he had never used it. But at the age of 96, he was ready, he was prepared, and when the need came, he used it. And this is what we see in the life of Daniel. We'll see this repeatedly as we finish this book, that even when he was older and had been in semiretirement, he was still prepared to serve when called upon.

Look at Daniel 5:14, "I have heard of you, that the Spirit of God is in you, and that light and understanding and excellent wisdom are found in you." Of course, he had heard that from his mother, but probably others reinforced that. But Daniel was sanctified for the purposes of God. And we'll see this as we continue, that his purpose was serving God and God alone. Let's continue in Daniel 5:15–16:

> "Now the wise men, the astrologers, have been brought in before me, that they should read this writing and make known to me its interpretation, but they could not give the interpretation of the thing. And I have heard of you, that you can give interpretations and explain enigmas. Now if you can read the writing and make known to me its interpretation, you shall be clothed with purple and have a chain of gold around your neck, and shall be the third ruler in the kingdom.'"

Now notice Daniel's response in Daniel 5:17, "Then Daniel answered, and said before the king, 'Let your gifts be for yourself, and give your rewards to another; yet I will read the writing to the king, and make known to him the interpretation.'" Don't miss this: Daniel's motives were above reproach. Daniel was not for sale. Daniel was not about advancing himself or enriching himself. He sought first the kingdom of God and His righteousness. And as a result, he received more. As Jesus said in Matthew 6:33, "Seek first the kingdom of God and His righteousness, and all these things shall be added to you."

Look at Daniel 5:18–21:

> "O king, the Most High God gave Nebuchadnezzar your father a kingdom and majesty, glory and honor. And because of the majesty that He gave him, all peoples, nations, and languages trembled and feared before him. Whomever he wished, he executed; whomever he wished, he kept alive; whomever he wished, he set up; and whomever he wished, he put down. But when his heart was lifted up, and his spirit was hardened in pride, he was deposed from his kingly throne, and they took his glory from him.

> Then he was driven from the sons of men, his heart was made like the beasts, and his dwelling was with the wild donkeys. They fed him with grass like oxen, and his body was wet with the dew of heaven, till he knew that the Most High God rules in the kingdom of men, and appoints over it whomever He chooses."

Nebuchadnezzar didn't teach this to his children, but now Daniel is giving him a history lesson and a lesson about pride. Continue reading in Daniel 5:22, "But you his son, Belshazzar, have not humbled your heart, although you knew all this." So now Daniel was saying Belshazzar should have known this. Maybe he was exposed to it, but he wasn't living it. See Daniel 5:23:

> "And you have lifted yourself up against the Lord of heaven. They have brought the vessels of His house before you, and you and your lords, your wives and your concubines, have drunk wine from them. And you have praised the gods of silver and gold, bronze and iron, wood and stone, which do not see or hear or know; and the God who holds your breath in His hand and owns all your ways, you have not glorified."

The downfall of individuals and nations is a progression. It doesn't happen right away, but it's rooted in pride, pride that ultimately profanes God and that which is holy.

Look at Daniel 5:24–25, "Then the fingers of the hand were sent from Him, and this writing was written. And this is the inscription that was written: MENE, MENE, TEKEL, UPHARSIN." Now, these are nouns in Aramaic, and the interpretation can be found in verb form in Daniel 5:26–28, "This is the interpretation of each word. MENE: God has numbered your kingdom, and finished it; TEKEL: You have been weighed in the balances, and found wanting; PERES: Your kingdom has been divided, and given to the Medes and Persians."

Let's continue in Daniel 5:29–31:

> Then Belshazzar gave the command, and they clothed Daniel with purple and put a chain of gold around his neck, and made a proclamation concerning him that he should be the third ruler in the kingdom.
>
> That very night Belshazzar, king of the Chaldeans, was slain. And Darius the Mede received the kingdom, being about sixty-two years old.

So, we can learn from Daniel how to solve the perplexing problems in a world where the handwriting, quite frankly, is on the wall. Here's what we learn:

1. He was prayerful and prepared to serve.
2. Pride had no place in his heart.
3. He was proficient and principled in his service, and he was a problem solver.
4. He provided clarity in a time of chaos and calamity.

And that's what we should seek: to be prayerful, prepared for service, pride having no place in our hearts, and to be proficient and principled in our service. We should also be problem solvers, having clarity in the times of chaos and calamity. And that comes by being in relationship with God, being in His Word, and being sanctified for the purposes that He has called us to.

Questions for Reflection and Discussion

1. What did King Belshazzar do to incur God's judgment (see vv. 2–4, 22–23)?

2. What interpretation of the mysterious words on the wall did Daniel give the king (see vv. 25–28)?
   a. MENE, "God has numbered [the days of] your kingdom" and brought it to an end.
   b. TEKEL, "You have been weighed in the balances, and found wanting."
   c. PERES, "Your kingdom has been divided, and given to the Medes and Persians."
   d. All of the above

Notes on Today's Bible Reading

Persian Empire

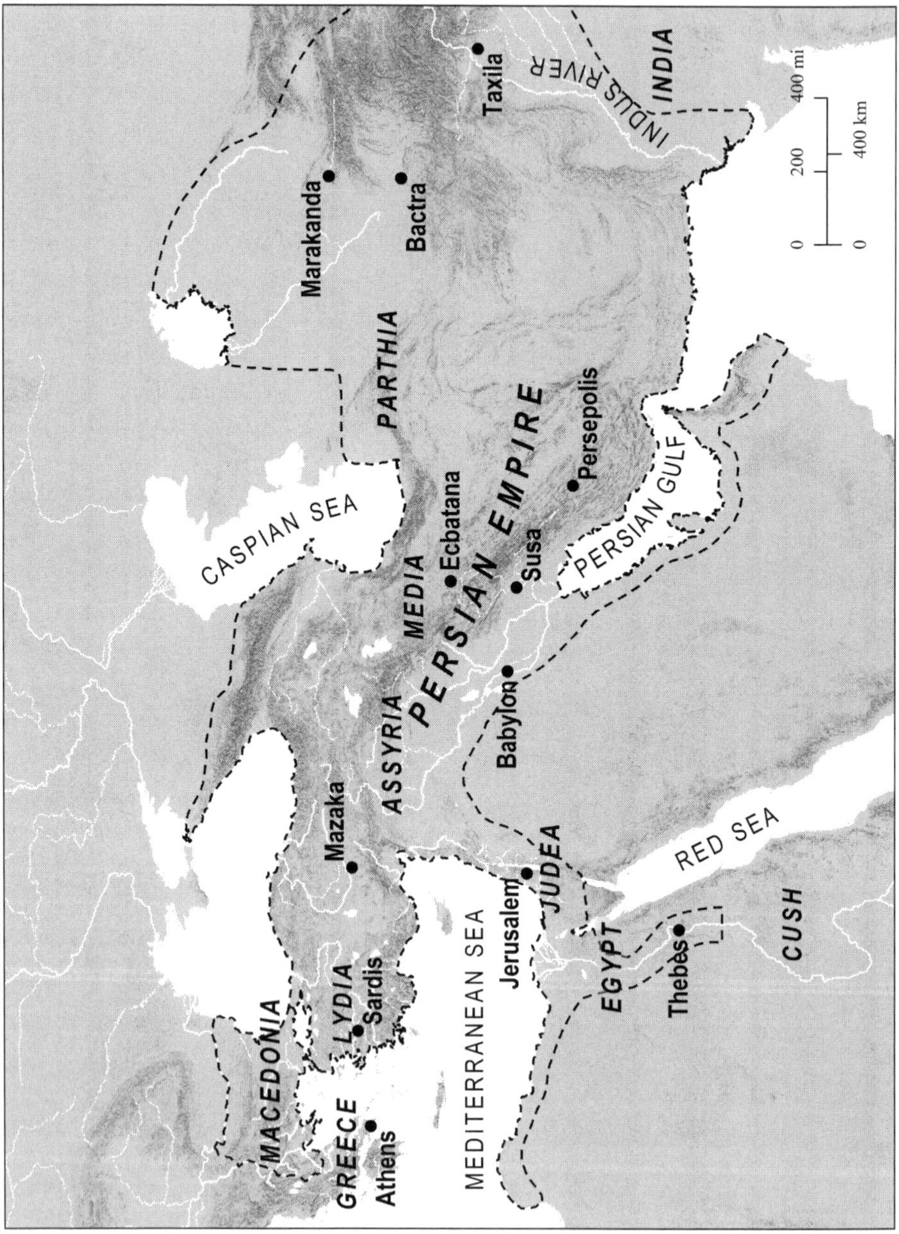

— Day 7 —

Today's Reading: Daniel 6

Verse of the Day

> All the governors of the kingdom, the administrators and satraps, the counselors and advisors, have consulted together to establish a royal statute and to make a firm decree, that whoever petitions any god or man for thirty days, except you, O king, shall be cast into the den of lions.
>
> — *Daniel 6:7*

Please read the entire Scripture selection in your own Bible and highlight or underline verses that stand out to you before you read the observations and engage the questions below.

Today we are in Daniel 6. The topic is "Bring in the Lions: When government takes the place of God." Our key verse is Daniel 6:7:

> "All the governors of the kingdom, the administrators and satraps, the counselors and advisors, have consulted together to establish a royal statute and to make a firm decree, that whoever petitions any god or man for thirty days, except you, O king, shall be cast into the den of lions."

Now the Bible stories about Daniel and the lions' den depict him as a child or a young man, but in reality, at this point in his life, he was over 70 years old. He served more than a half-dozen different rulers over his career. He served six kings, one co-regent, and one governor.

This event took place after Babylon fell to the Medes and the Persians. While the historical records are inconclusive, Daniel served under Darius, who is here considered a governor under Cyrus. Daniel not only served from Babylonian administration to administration, but was elevated under Darius after Babylon was conquered. How did Daniel manage to do this? How did he survive one hostile administration after another? His focus was on serving God. He didn't jockey for position. He wasn't looking for power. He was simply obedient to God, and he served Him.

We see that reflected over in Daniel 5:16–17 when Belshazzar called him out of semiretirement to interpret the handwriting on the wall. We read:

> "And I have heard of you, that you can give interpretations and explain enigmas. Now if you can read the writing and make known to me its interpretation, you shall be clothed with purple and have a chain of gold around your neck, and shall be the third ruler in the kingdom."
>
> Then Daniel answered, and said before the king, "Let your gifts be for yourself, and give your rewards to another; yet I will read the writing to the king, and make known to him the interpretation."

He basically said, "Keep your gifts. That's not why I'm here. I will do what you ask because I serve God. I'm not interested in the things that you have to offer me." This wasn't arrogance or a condescending view. It's simply that Daniel's eyes were fixed elsewhere.

We are told to do the same. Look what Paul wrote in Colossians 3:1–2, "If then you were raised with Christ, seek those things which are above, where Christ is, sitting at the right hand of God. Set your mind on things above, not on things on the earth." So, he was saying, "Look, if you're a follower of Jesus Christ, your eyes need to be where Jesus is. Your affections need to be where He is, at the right hand of God. You need to be focused on those things in heaven, not the things here on this earth."

OK, so let's look now at Daniel 6:1–3:

> It pleased Darius to set over the kingdom one hundred and twenty satraps, to be over the whole kingdom; and over these, three governors, of whom Daniel was one, that the satraps might give account to them, so that the king would suffer no loss. Then this Daniel distinguished himself above the governors and satraps, because an excellent spirit was in him; and the king gave thought to setting him over the whole realm.

Here's the picture. There were three governors, but Daniel exceeded those other two, and there was an excellent spirit in him. As followers of Jesus Christ, that should describe us as well. We should serve with excellence. And Daniel's excellence was such that the king wanted to put him over the other two, so he would be at the very top.

Let's continue in Daniel 6:4, "So the governors and satraps sought to find some charge against Daniel concerning the kingdom; but they could find no charge or fault, because he was faithful; nor was there any error or fault found in him." They wanted to try to bring him down, but they couldn't find a reason because he was faithful. He served with excellence. We continue in Daniel 6:5, "Then these men said, 'We shall not find any charge against this Daniel unless we find it against him concerning the law of his God.'"

So, they realized Daniel was committed to his God and that they would have to set a trap for him. Look at Daniel 6:6–7:

> So these governors and satraps thronged before the king, and said thus to him: "King Darius, live forever! All the governors of the kingdom, the administrators and satraps, the counselors and advisors, have consulted together to establish a royal statute and to make a firm decree, that whoever petitions any god or man for thirty days, except you, O king, shall be cast into the den of lions."

Now I have to wonder, where was Daniel in this? Why didn't the king talk to Daniel? We don't know. But Daniel 6:8 says, "Now, O king, establish the decree and sign the writing, so that it cannot be changed, according to the law of the Medes and Persians, which does not alter." Maybe Daniel was out of town. Maybe he was on a mission. Who knows?

Look at Daniel 6:9–11:

> Therefore King Darius signed the written decree.
>
> Now when Daniel knew that the writing was signed, he went home. And in his upper room, with his windows open toward Jerusalem, he knelt down on his knees three times that day, and prayed and gave thanks before his God, as was his custom since early days.

> Then these men assembled and found Daniel praying and making supplication before his God.

They could not find any fault with Daniel's work that might stop his rise and influence, so they devised to elevate government above God. Now, that begins to sound awfully familiar. These men sought to exclude followers of God not just from government service, but from society itself. They were essentially setting a trap for Daniel where they said, "If you want to do business, if you want to serve in government, your God can't be involved. First, you've got to show submission to the government." They knew that his devotion to God would cause him to come in conflict with the government.

So, what did Daniel do? When this order, this ordinance, was put out, he didn't shrink away or go silent, nor did he make a show. He did what was his custom or his practice. From his youth, he had prayed to God three times a day with his windows open. He wasn't hiding it. He didn't go into a secret place. He did what he had been doing. He rightfully sought to have his obedience to God accommodated by the government. He faithfully served. Humble obedience to God can never be wrong even when it violates the edicts of men. Now notice something else: Daniel did not provoke anyone. He didn't have what I call a "Jesus chip" on his shoulder, daring someone to knock it off.

Daniel simply did what he had always done. He didn't change. So what was the outcome? Well, it was more adversity. He did indeed face the lions. But as Daniel testified in Daniel 6:22,

> "My God sent His angel and shut the lions' mouths, so that they have not hurt me, because I was found innocent before Him; and also, O king, I have done no wrong before you."

But there was more. Not only did God bless Daniel for his humble obedience, but also for his willingness to face the consequences. Daniel disobeyed a government that had usurped the role of God, and God protected him miraculously. This led Darius, the ruler, to establish the recognition of this one true God as the standard.

Look at Daniel 6:25–26:

> Then King Darius wrote:
> To all peoples, nations, and languages that dwell in all the earth:
> Peace be multiplied to you.
> I make a decree that in every dominion of my kingdom
> men must tremble and fear before the God of Daniel.
> For He is the living God,
> And steadfast forever;
> His kingdom is the one which shall not be destroyed,
> And His dominion shall endure to the end.

When government takes the place of God and the effort is made to exclude followers of Christ from society, as we see happening today, we should seek and expect the accommodation of our faith while continuing to obey God and His Word. We serve the Lord, engage government, and then we watch with hopeful anticipation how God might use government to establish the rightful recognition that is due to the Lord Jesus Christ. Now, that does not mean that it won't come without adversity and difficulty and challenges, but nonetheless, we are to be obedient to God. We ought to obey God rather than man (Acts 5:29).

Questions for Reflection and Discussion

1. When government leaders cunningly convinced Persian King Darius to execute anyone who petitioned any god or others besides the king for thirty days, what did Daniel do (see vv. 10–11)?

2. What confession did the king make when God delivered Daniel from the lions?
   a. I knew I should not have fed those lions before tossing you in there.
   b. Obviously, you are so old and bony that the lions didn't see any need to bother.
   c. Daniel's God is the living God, enduring forever; His kingdom shall never be destroyed, and His dominion shall be to the end. He delivers and rescues; He works signs and wonders in heaven and on earth, He who has saved Daniel from the power of the lions.
   d. None of the above.

Notes on Today's Bible Reading

— Day 8 —

Today's Reading: Daniel 7

Verse of the Day

> "Then the kingdom and dominion,
> And the greatness of the kingdoms under the whole
>   heaven,
> Shall be given to the people, the saints of the Most High.
> His kingdom shall be an everlasting kingdom,
> And all dominions shall serve and obey Him."
>
> — ***Daniel 7:27***

Please read the entire Scripture selection in your own Bible and highlight or underline verses that stand out to you before you read the observations and engage the questions below.

Today we're in Daniel 7. The first six chapters of Daniel were primarily historical with prophecy mixed in, but the remaining six chapters are strictly focused on prophecy and can be difficult to understand. These last six chapters leave even the greatest biblical scholars differing in their interpretations and their understanding. I'm going to stay at the 30,000-foot level with a general thematic overview of this chapter.

You'll notice that these chapters are not in chronological order. Chronologically, the events in Daniel 7 took place before the events in Daniel 5. Again, the chapters are grouped together because they're focused on what was to come, and that's the prophecy. Now the vision or dream that Daniel had here in Daniel 7 really runs parallel to Nebuchadnezzar's dream from Daniel 2 of the four kingdoms reaching to the millennial reign of Christ.

Let's begin in Daniel 7:1–8:

> In the first year of Belshazzar king of Babylon, Daniel had a dream and visions of his head while on his bed. Then he wrote down the dream, telling the main facts.
>
> Daniel spoke, saying, "I saw in my vision by night, and behold, the four winds of heaven were stirring up the Great Sea. And four great beasts came up from the sea, each different from the other. The first was like a lion, and had eagle's wings. I watched till its wings were plucked off; and it was lifted up from the earth and made to stand on two feet like a man, and a man's heart was given to it.
>
> "And suddenly another beast, a second, like a bear. It was raised up on one side, and had three ribs in its mouth between its teeth. And they said thus to it: 'Arise, devour much flesh!'
>
> "After this I looked, and there was another, like a leopard, which had on its back four wings of a bird. The beast also had four heads, and dominion was given to it.
>
> "After this I saw in the night visions, and behold, a fourth beast, dreadful and terrible, exceedingly strong. It had huge iron teeth; it was devouring, breaking in pieces, and trampling the residue with its feet. It was different from all the beasts that were before it, and it had ten horns.

I was considering the horns, and there was another horn, a little one, coming up among them, before whom three of the first horns were plucked out by the roots. And there, in this horn, were eyes like the eyes of a man, and a mouth speaking pompous words."

Now let's drop down to Daniel 7:21–25:

"I was watching; and the same horn was making war against the saints, and prevailing against them, until the Ancient of Days came, and a judgment was made in favor of the saints of the Most High, and the time came for the saints to possess the kingdom.

"Thus he said:

'The fourth beast shall be
A fourth kingdom on earth,
Which shall be different from all other kingdoms,
And shall devour the whole earth,
Trample it and break it in pieces.
The ten horns are ten kings
Who shall arise from this kingdom.
And another shall rise after them;
He shall be different from the first ones,
And shall subdue three kings.
He shall speak pompous words against the Most High,
Shall persecute the saints of the Most High,
and shall intend to change times and law.
Then the saints shall be given into his hand
For a time and times and half a time.'"

The four kingdoms here are the Chaldeans or the Babylonians (which Nebuchadnezzar began), the Medes and the Persians, the Grecian Empire, and, finally, the Roman Empire. Now this final empire and ruler is a subject of much debate. Many Bible scholars see the ultimate fulfillment of the final horn as the end times' Antichrist.

Now let's look back at Daniel 7:19–21:

> "Then I wished to know the truth about the fourth beast, which was different from all the others, exceedingly dreadful, with its teeth of iron and its nails of bronze, which devoured, broke in pieces, and trampled the residue with its feet; and the ten horns that were on its head, and the other horn which came up, before which three fell, namely, that horn which had eyes and a mouth which spoke pompous words, whose appearance was greater than his fellows.
>
> "I was watching; and the same horn was making war against the saints, and prevailing against them, until the Ancient of Days came, and a judgment was made in favor of the saints of the Most High, and the time came for the saints to possess the kingdom."

Let's look at what Paul had to say about the final war and the Antichrist in 2 Thessalonians 2:1–2, "Now, brethren, concerning the coming of our Lord Jesus Christ and our gathering together to Him, we ask you, not to be soon shaken in mind or troubled, either by spirit or by word or by letter, as if from us, as though the day of Christ had come." In other words, Paul was saying, "Don't get upset about what's happening around you or what you hear." Now look at 2 Thessalonians 2:3–4:

> Let no one deceive you by any means; for that Day will not come unless the falling away comes first, and the man of sin is revealed, the son of perdition, who opposes and exalts himself above all that is called God or that is worshiped, so that he sits as God in the temple of God, showing himself that he is God.

Let's look back at what this final horn was doing. It was speaking against God. It was changing the laws and the times. Read further in 2 Thessalonians 2:5–7: "Do you not remember that when I was still with you I told you these things? And now you know what is restraining, that he may be revealed in his own time. For the mystery of lawlessness is already at work; only He who now restrains will do so until He is taken out of the way." Who is restraining the lawless one today, even though we see lawlessness expanding? This is the spirit of lawlessness of this age that is moving forward in preparation ultimately for the Antichrist to come forth. The Holy Spirit, present in the people of God restrains the lawless one. When will the Holy Spirit leave? It will leave when the church is raptured out and taken away. Then the lawless one will have his way.

I think we already see this at work as Paul said in 2 Thessalonians 2:7–8, "For the mystery of lawlessness is already at work; only He who now restrains will do so until He is taken out of the way. And then the lawless one will be revealed, whom the Lord will consume with the breath of His mouth and destroy with the brightness of His coming." This is what was contained in Daniel's vision. The coming of the lawless one is by the activity of Satan. Paul offers further affirmation of this understanding in 2 Thessalonians 2:9–10, "The coming of the lawless one is according to the working of Satan, with all power, signs, and lying wonders, and with all unrighteous deception among those who perish, because they did not receive the love of the truth, that they might be saved." They rejected the truth of God, so they were deceived, as Romans 1 talks about. Let's go back to Daniel 7:9a, "I watched till thrones were put in place, and the Ancient of Days was seated…" There is coming a day when the judgment will take place. And this is what we read in verses 9b–10:

> "His garment was white as snow,
> And the hair of His head was like pure wool.
> His throne was a fiery flame,
> Its wheels a burning fire;
> A fiery stream issued
> And came forth from before Him.
> A thousand thousands ministered to Him;
> Ten thousand times ten thousand stood before Him.
> The court was seated,
> And the books were opened."

The bottom line here is that man has his day, but God has eternity. There is a King who is coming.

Now let's read Daniel 7:13–14:

> "I was watching in the night visions,
> And behold, One like the Son of Man,
> Coming with the clouds of heaven!
> He came to the Ancient of Days,
> And they brought Him near before Him.
> Then to Him was given dominion and glory and a kingdom,
> That all peoples, nations, and languages should serve Him.

His dominion is an everlasting dominion,
Which shall not pass away,
And His kingdom the one
Which shall not be destroyed."

You see, in these visions of these four kingdoms, each one of them passed away, and there was a successive empire that arose for a time. With Jesus Christ, when His kingdom is set up, it will be forever and ever.

As we look at this prophecy and what Paul wrote, note that opposition and persecution have been the experience of the church for 2,000 years. It's the reality of the spiritual battle that is raging around us whether we acknowledge it or not. Let me ask you this question: Are these prophetic words that open our eyes to the reality of this battle intended to discourage us? No, on the contrary! Notice what Jesus told His disciples over in John 16:33, "These things I have spoken to you, that in Me you may have peace. In the world you will have tribulation; but be of good cheer, I have overcome the world."

This prophecy was intended to tell us, "Look, there will be difficult times." What we see happening in America today or what we see happening around the world is that reality Scripture speaks of. We are in difficult times now. We've enjoyed peaceful times, and that's great. I'd love to have more of them, and maybe we will. But the reality is that there is a spiritual battle raging, and the lawless one is working his way toward that climactic day. Yet even in the midst of this, we can have peace because the Kingdom of God is already being established not by geographical boundaries of countries or empires, but it's already being established in the hearts and minds of men, women, and children.

There is a physical Kingdom coming, but now it's being established spiritually in the hearts and minds of people. Jesus and this prophecy both tell us that difficult days will be upon us, but the day is coming when the Kingdom of God will reign forever and ever and ever. And we should take heart and find encouragement in that. There will be no end to the Kingdom of Jesus Christ. Those by faith who accept the grace that God has extended to us and trust Jesus Christ as Lord and Savior are citizens of that Kingdom. No matter what happens today, tomorrow, or next year, nothing will shake that Kingdom.

Questions for Reflection and Discussion

1. How did Daniel describe the coming of the Son of Man, Jesus (see vv. 13–14)?
   a. He comes with the clouds of heaven.
   b. Dominion is given so that all will serve Him.
   c. His dominion will be everlasting.
   d. All of the above

2. What did Daniel say about the blasphemous beast and what will happen to his dominion (see vv. 24–27)?

Notes on Today's Bible Reading

Greek Empire under Alexander the Great

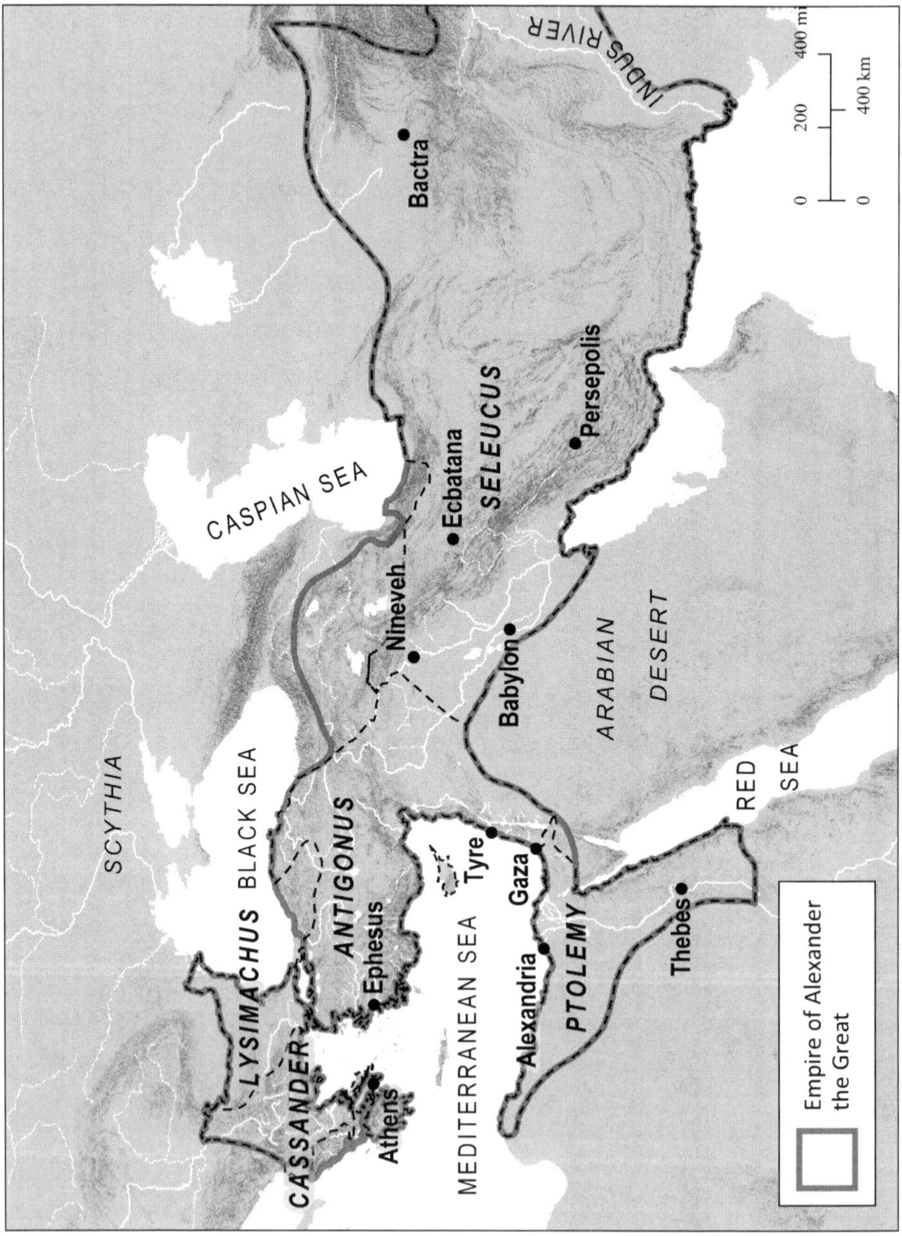

— Day 9 —

Today's Reading: Daniel 8

Verse of the Day

> "And I, Daniel, fainted and was sick for days; afterward I arose and went about the king's business. I was astonished by the vision, but no one understood it."
>
> — *Daniel 8:27*

Please read the entire Scripture selection in your own Bible and highlight or underline verses that stand out to you before you read the observations and engage the questions below.

Today we are in Daniel 8, and we are going to talk about the ram charger. Our key verse is Daniel 8:27, "And I, Daniel, fainted and was sick for days; afterward I arose and went about the king's business. I was astonished by the vision, but no one understood it." If you're trying to figure out this prophecy and it doesn't make a whole lot of sense to you, don't feel bad. You are not alone. Even Daniel had a hard time with it. This vision moves us closer to the second and the third world empires that we first saw in chapter 2 and then in chapter 7. So, this zeros in on the kingdom of the Medes and the Persians and the empire of Greece. Now, the primary audience also shifted because he moved from writing in Aramaic to Hebrew in chapter 8. Consequently, the audience here was primarily Jewish people. Most scholars see this prophecy as having been fulfilled. However, there are also some who also see it as symbolic of what is yet to come, as a type or a shadow. I agree with this latter view, and we'll talk more about that in a moment.

Let's start in Daniel 8:1–2:

> In the third year of the reign of King Belshazzar a vision appeared to me—to me, Daniel—after the one that appeared to me the first time. I saw in the vision, and it so happened while I was looking, that I was in Shushan, the citadel, which is in the province of Elam; and I saw in the vision that I was by the River Ulai.

By the way, Susa would become the capital of the kingdom under Cyrus, when this prophecy was in the process of being fulfilled. Let's continue in Daniel 8:3: "Then I lifted my eyes and saw, and there, standing beside the river, was a ram which had two horns, and the two horns were high; but one was higher than the other, and the higher one came up last." Now this ram represents the Medes and the Persians, and the higher of the two horns is Persia. Media and Persia initially worked together, but Cyrus the Persian took control in 550 BC.

Look at Daniel 8:4–5:

> I saw the ram pushing westward, northward, and southward, so that no animal could withstand him; nor was there any that could deliver from his hand, but he did according to his will and became great.
>
> And as I was considering, suddenly a male goat came from the west, across the surface of the whole earth,

> without touching the ground; and the goat had a notable horn between his eyes.

Daniel saw a "flying goat" in this vision, Some might think he just had a bad piece of Persian pizza. Seriously, this is a prophecy about Alexander the Great and his Greek Empire. In the previous vision, Greece was a four-headed leopard with four wings (Daniel 7:6). Both of these visions speak to how swiftly Alexander moved his army. The ability to move an army rapidly is a tremendous tactical advantage in battle. Some of the greatest military leaders in world history had this ability to move with great speed, which led to success. Joshua moved his men through the night (Joshua 10:9) and over great distances very quickly, and God granted them victory. In fact, Joshua was studied by many great generals. In the Civil War, Stonewall Jackson also moved his men rapidly over great distances through the night, achieving the element of surprise. General Patton in World War II was known for moving quickly over great distances as well. Point is that this prophecy foretells the "blitzkrieg" tactics of Alexander the Great, who is considered one of the world's greatest military strategists and generals.

Look at Daniel 8:6–8:

> Then he [the flying goat] came to the ram that had two horns, which I had seen standing beside the river, and ran at him with furious power. And I saw him confronting the ram; he was moved with rage against him, attacked the ram, and broke his two horns. There was no power in the ram to withstand him, but he cast him down to the ground and trampled him; and there was no one that could deliver the ram from his hand.

> Therefore the male goat grew very great; but when he became strong, the large horn was broken, and in place of it four notable ones came up toward the four winds of heaven.

Just as the prophecy foretold, Alexander the Great, the large horn, died at the zenith of his success. He was only 32, maybe 33 years old. After his death, the vast empire which he had created was divided among his four generals (the four horns): Cassander, Lysimachus, Seleucus, and Ptolemy. And those four divided up all the territory that he had. Look at Daniel 8:9, "And out of one of them came a little horn which grew exceedingly great toward the south, toward the east, and toward the Glorious Land." The land referred to here is Israel. This little horn is not the little horn in chapter 7 that comes in after the fourth empire. This little horn refers to Antiochus Epiphanes IV, who arose as the ruler of the northern Seleucid Empire in 175 BC.

Now, let's continue in Daniel 8:10–12:

> And it [the little horn] grew up to the host of heaven; and it cast down some of the host and some of the stars to the ground, and trampled them. He even exalted himself as high as the Prince of the host; and by him the daily sacrifices were taken away, and the place of His sanctuary was cast down. Because of transgression, an army was given over to the horn to oppose the daily sacrifices; and he cast truth down to the ground. He did all this and prospered.

Now, this is a bit confusing, but the bottom line is that Antiochus was evil. And as we'll see in just a moment, Antiochus was a type of Antichrist. His genocidal efforts, quite frankly, were in alignment with Hitler's pogrom against the Jews. Antiochus wanted to eliminate the Jewish culture, the Jewish religion, and the Jewish people. He tried first to Hellenize them in order to "cleanse" them. He burned all the scrolls of the Torah. He desecrated the temple by sacrificing a pig on the altar and then putting a statue of Zeus in the temple. His evil and vicious rule fueled the Maccabean Revolt.

Look at Daniel 8:13–18:

> Then I heard a holy one speaking; and another holy one said to that certain one who was speaking, "How long will the vision be, concerning the daily sacrifices and the transgression of desolation, the giving of both the sanctuary and the host to be trampled underfoot?"
>
> And he said to me, "For two thousand three hundred days; then the sanctuary shall be cleansed."
>
> Then it happened, when I, Daniel, had seen the vision and was seeking the meaning, that suddenly there stood before me one having the appearance of a man. And I heard a man's voice between the banks of the Ulai, who called, and said, "Gabriel, make this man understand the vision. So he came near where I stood, and when he came I was afraid and fell on my face; but he said to me, "Understand, son of man, that the vision refers to the time of the end."
>
> Now, as he was speaking with me, I was in a deep sleep with my face to the ground; but he touched me, and stood me upright.

Obviously, Daniel was dealing with the angel Gabriel, and he responded with understandable fear and reverence.

Look at Daniel 8:19, "And he said, 'Look, I am making known to you what shall happen in the latter time of the indignation; for at the appointed time the end shall be.'" Now, for the rest of the chapter here, Gabriel explained this dream to Daniel. First, he explained the 2,300 evening and morning offerings. If you count two offerings per day, this is just over three years. Now, if you had just one offering per day, then that's about six years and three months or so. But if you look at this as two offerings per day, this is just a little over three years, which was the time between the desecration of the temple by Antiochus and the Maccabees defeating Antiochus and cleansing the temple. This act of cleansing the temple and the Jewish people reestablishing their own sovereignty for a while is commemorated each year in the Jewish celebration of Hanukkah.

Drop down to Daniel 8:24–25:

> "His power shall be mighty, but not by his own power;
> He shall destroy fearfully,
> And shall prosper and thrive;
> He shall destroy the mighty, and also the holy people.
>
> "Through his cunning
> He shall cause deceit to prosper under his rule;
> And he shall exalt himself in his heart.
> He shall destroy many in their prosperity.
> He shall even rise against the Prince of princes;
> But he shall be broken without human means."

Now, I want us to look at verse 25 in the NIV because it's a little bit different. In fact, almost every translation has this verse different from every other. In the NIV, Daniel 8:25 says, "He [a fierce-looking king] will cause deceit to prosper, and he will consider himself superior. When they feel secure, he will destroy many and take his stand against the Prince of princes. Yet he will be destroyed, but not by human power." There are a couple of things to take note of here in the NKJV. The first is where it says, "His [the king's] power shall be mighty, but not by his own power" (v. 24).

Now, there are two things we need to understand from this. One is that God is the One who allows this for a time. And the second is that the power is not from Him, but it is demonic. Just like the coming Antichrist, this king is powered from below. He is cunning. Deceitfulness will abound during his reign. Pride and arrogance define him. He is opposed to God, directly against God, and against the things of God, throwing down the truth.

So, let's go back to Antiochus for just a moment for another important fulfillment. We read that this evil leader will be destroyed, but not by the hand of man. Antiochus was not killed in battle. He died a painful death from internal parasites. He did not die by the hand of man. So, he fit this picture. But here's the takeaway: Antiochus is a type and a foreshadowing of the Antichrist, who will be given the ability to destroy for a set period of time. He will take on God.

You know, we see this over and over. There's a recognition that history repeats itself. We've seen this attack on the Jewish people from Antiochus, Roman rulers, Hitler, and we have seen a rise of antisemitism in recent days. History repeats itself because, as Paul described in Ephesians 6, those powers of darkness continue to manipulate and lead fallen, unredeemed people to carry out their deeds of darkness. And that doesn't change.

Let's look at the final verse. Daniel 8:27, "And I, Daniel, fainted and was sick for days; afterward I arose and went about the king's business. I was astonished by the vision, but no one understood it." The receipt of this vision weighed heavy on Daniel, so much so it made him ill. End-time prophecy is especially heavy. We don't know exactly when and how every detail of it is going to be fulfilled. We see the types, the patterns, and some of the signs, we just need to pray that the Holy Spirit leads us to understand what we need to know for the time in which we live.

Questions for Reflection and Discussion

1. Which angel explained the vision to Daniel (see v. 16)?
   a. Michael
   b. Gabriel
   c. Abaddon
   d. None of the above

2. What animals did Daniel see in his vision, and what nations did they represent (see vv. 20–25)?

Notes on Today's Bible Reading

— Day 10 —

Today's Reading: Daniel 9

Verse of the Day

> "He informed me, and talked with me, and said, 'O Daniel, I have now come forth to give you skill to understand.'"
>
> — *Daniel 9:22*

Please read the entire Scripture selection in your own Bible and highlight or underline verses that stand out to you before you read the observations and engage the questions below.

If you're a numbers person, you'll like Daniel 9. The topic is the 70 weeks of years. Our key verse is Daniel 9:22, "He informed me, and talked with me, and said, 'O Daniel, I have now come forth to give you skill to understand.'" The angel Gabriel, one of only two good angels mentioned by name in the Bible, was dispatched with an answer to Daniel's prayer and to give Daniel the ability to understand what was to come.

Most of the prophecy in this chapter has been fulfilled already. There are differing views and interpretations, as with much of Bible prophecy, so please feel free to disagree with me on the prophetic aspects of this passage. As I have stated before, Bible prophecy is very important. We shouldn't skip over it. We should read it, study it, and strive to understand it. But we should approach it with both caution and humility because its meaning is not always crystal clear. That said, there are some very relevant and important principles in this passage that have direct application to our lives today, and that's going to be my primary focus.

Let's start in Daniel 9:1–2:

> In the first year of Darius the son of Ahasuerus, of the lineage of the Medes, who was made king over the realm of the Chaldeans—in the first year of his reign I, Daniel, understood by the books the number of the years specified by the word of the LORD through Jeremiah the prophet, that He would accomplish seventy years in the desolations of Jerusalem.

The year was probably 538 BC before Daniel was thrown into the lions' den, which gives us some additional insight into what led to the events of chapter 6. Now Daniel realized from the writings of Jeremiah that the time of captivity as promised by God was up. And this may be why he was so committed to prayer and why there was opposition to his prayer back in chapter 6, he was appealing to God to fulfill His word.

Let's continue in Daniel 9:3–5:

> Then I set my face toward the LORD God to make request by prayer and supplications, with fasting, sackcloth, and ashes. And I prayed to the LORD my God, and made confession, and said, "O Lord, great and awesome God, who keeps His covenant and mercy with those who love Him, and with those who keep His commandments, we have

> sinned and committed iniquity, we have done wickedly and rebelled, even by departing from Your precepts and Your judgments."

Now, as we read through this, it sounds very much like the prayer of Nehemiah. Daniel, like Nehemiah, identified with the sins of the people and confessed them before God, being very specific about how they had rebelled against God and His ways. Look at Daniel 9:6–7:

> "Neither have we heeded Your servants the prophets, who spoke in Your name to our kings and our princes, to our fathers and all the people of the land. O Lord, righteousness belongs to You, but to us shame of face, as it is this day—to the men of Judah, to the inhabitants of Jerusalem and all Israel, those near and those far off in all the countries to which You have driven them, because of the unfaithfulness which they have committed against You."

What Daniel said next is no surprise: "The result of our disobedience is exactly what your word said it would be." Now this is genuine repentance. What we see here is that Daniel did not shift the blame. He owned up to the wrong that he had done. Look at Daniel 9:13–15:

> "As it is written in the Law of Moses, all this disaster has come upon us; yet we have not made our prayer before the LORD our God, that we might turn from our iniquities and understand Your truth. Therefore the LORD has kept the disaster in mind, and brought it upon us; for the LORD our

> God is righteous in all the works which He does, though we have not obeyed His voice. And now, O Lord our God, who brought Your people out of the land of Egypt with a mighty hand, and made Yourself a name, as it is this day—we have sinned, we have done wickedly!"

Drop down to Daniel 9:17–19:

> "Now therefore, our God, hear the prayer of Your servant, and his supplications, and for the Lord's sake cause Your face to shine on Your sanctuary, which is desolate. O my God, incline Your ear and hear; open Your eyes and see our desolations, and the city which is called by Your name; for we do not present our supplications before You because of our righteous deeds, but because of Your great mercies. O Lord, hear! O Lord, forgive! O Lord, listen and act! Do not delay for Your own sake, my God, for Your city and Your people are called by Your name."

So, here are five points that we see from this great prayer that Daniel prays:

Number 1: It's based upon God's greatness. It's not based upon their standing, who they are. It's based upon God's greatness.

Number 2: It's based upon God's covenant, His promises.

Number 3: It's based upon God's history with them. He brought them out of the land of Egypt. He has shown His power before. He has sustained them.

Number 4: It's based upon God's name. We've talked about that before: we appeal to the name of God. And that's what Daniel's doing here. He's appealing to the reputation of God.

Number 5: We see it's based upon God's mercy.

Next, we move into the prophetic part of this chapter. The first part was easy. Now we get into the more challenging part. Look at Daniel 9:20–23:

> Now while I was speaking, praying, and confessing my sin and the sin of my people Israel, and presenting my supplication before the LORD my God for the holy mountain of my God, yes, while I was speaking in prayer, the man Gabriel, whom I had seen in the vision at the beginning, being caused to fly swiftly, reached me about the time of the evening offering. And he informed me, and talked with me, and said, "O Daniel, I have now come forth to give you skill to understand. At the beginning of your supplications the command went out, and I have come to tell you, for you are greatly beloved; therefore consider the matter, and understand the vision."

While Daniel was praying, God dispatched Gabriel with a message. Look at Daniel 9:24:

> "Seventy weeks are determined
> For your people and for your holy city,
> To finish the transgression,
> To make an end of sins,

To make reconciliation for iniquity,
To bring in everlasting righteousness,
To seal up vision and prophecy,
And to anoint the Most Holy."

Many scholars point to this passage as one of the strongest in the Old Testament supporting Jesus as the Messiah. So, quoting from *Halley's Bible Handbook*: "The 70 weeks is generally understood to mean 70 weeks of years. That is, 70 sevens of years or seven times 70, which is 490 years."[3] Let's continue with Daniel 9:25:

"Know therefore and understand,
That from the going forth of the command
To restore and build Jerusalem
Until Messiah the Prince,
There shall be seven weeks and sixty-two weeks;
The street shall be built again, and the wall,
Even in troublesome times."

Just to note, "troublesome times" are what we find throughout most of our walk with the Lord. It's going to be a troubled time moving forward to the end. And it says that a lot of this is going to happen in a troubled time.

Now, this is where we start to get differing opinions and interpretations of the 490 years. Let's see if we can make sense of the "70 weeks of years." We see it here in the subsequent verses: 7 weeks, 62 weeks, and 1 week. Now, the significance of the 7 weeks is not immediately clear, but if you add the 7 weeks to the 62 weeks, you have 483 years. Again, quoting from Halley:

> This 483 years is the period between the decree to rebuild Jerusalem and the coming of the Anointed One . . . . The decree to rebuild Jerusalem was 458 BC. Adding 483 years to 457 BC brings us to AD 26, the very year in which Jesus was baptized and began His public ministry. A most remarkable fulfillment of Daniel's prophecy, even to the year.[4]

Let's continue in Daniel 9:26–27:

> "And after the sixty-two weeks
> Messiah shall be cut off, but not for Himself;
> And the people of the prince who is to come
> Shall destroy the city and the sanctuary.
> The end of it shall be with a flood,
> And till the end of the war desolations are determined.
> Then he shall confirm a covenant with many for one week;
> But in the middle of the week
> He shall bring an end to sacrifice and offering.
> And on the wing of abominations shall be one who makes desolate,
> Even until the consummation, which is determined,
> Is poured out on the desolate."

So, what is this prophecy communicating here? Again, I quote from Halley:

> [W]ithin 3½ years Jesus was crucified, that is, "in the middle of the 'sevens'" (in the middle of the week) "the Anointed One" was "put to death"; He atoned for wickedness and

> brought in everlasting righteousness (vv. 24, 26–27). Thus Daniel foretold not only the time at which the Messiah would appear, but also the duration of His public ministry and His atoning death for human sin.[5]

The Messiah's once-for-all sacrifice puts an end to the need for further sacrifices.

Regarding the remaining half of the 70th week, the interpretations go in various directions, as Halley further explains:

> Some think that the remaining half of the 70th week was completed in the few years after Christ's death and resurrection. Others believe that the fulfillment of the 70th week was suspended at the death and resurrection of Christ and will remain suspended as long as Israel is scattered; the last half of the "one week" then belongs to the time of the end.
>
> Yet another viewpoint is that there is an indeterminate interval between the 69th and 70th weeks. Some believe that the 70th week will begin at Christ's second coming and the rapture of the church. This, then, marks the beginning of the seven years referred to as the Great Tribulation period. It is thought that during this time the "little horn" of chapter 8 will rise to power and enter into a seven-year covenant with the Jews (Israel). This covenant is then broken after 3½ years and the remaining 3½ years represent a time of great war and destruction, leading up to the great and final battle of Armageddon. (See Revelation 7:14 regarding the tribulation period.)[6]

As you can see, it's very challenging to understand these prophecies with certainty, but it's essential that we do try our very best to understand what the Lord is communicating through His word about End-Time prophecy. One aspect we should all be able to agree upon is that we need to stand on God's word and be ready for His return.

Questions for Reflection and Discussion

1. When Daniel searched the prophecies of Jeremiah and realized the exile would last seventy years, he cried out to God for mercy (see v. 3). What can we learn from his prayer (vv. 4–19) about how we should pray for America?

2. How did God respond to Daniel's cry for mercy (see vv. 20–27)?
   a. Sent Gabriel with an encouraging personal message
   b. Gave Daniel the interpretation to the vision of the end times
   c. Both of the above

Notes on Today's Bible Reading

— Day 11 —

Today's Reading: Daniel 10

Verse of the Day

> "The prince of the kingdom of Persia withstood me twenty-one days; and behold, Michael, one of the chief princes, came to help me, for I had been left alone there with the kings of Persia."
>
> — *Daniel 10:13*

Please read the entire Scripture selection in your own Bible and highlight or underline verses that stand out to you before you read the observations and engage the questions below.

Daniel 10 is an amazing chapter. Our key verse is Daniel 10:13, "But the prince of the kingdom of Persia withstood me twenty-one days; and behold, Michael, one of the chief princes, came to help me, for I had been left alone there with the kings of Persia." Now the next three chapters, the final chapters of Daniel, all go together. In chapter 10, we have Daniel's final recorded vision, and then in chapters 11 and 12 we have the explanation.

Before we get to that vision, let's remember our timeline with Daniel. He was taken captive by King Nebuchadnezzar's invasion force in 605 BC. He served under several Babylonian kings until

November of 539 BC, when Babylon fell to the Medes and the Persians. Daniel was set up as one of the three governors. In 538 BC, Daniel discovered the prophecy of Jeremiah that after 70 years of captivity, the Jewish people would return to Jerusalem. He prayed in chapter 9, asking God to act for His Name's sake. Now, we don't know this for certain, but this was most likely when Daniel's political adversaries managed to get the king to sign a decree that no one could petition anyone or any god except the king, which led to the lions' den incident and God's deliverance of Daniel. Shortly thereafter a decree was issued that the Jewish captives could return to Jerusalem. As we'll see later in Ezra and Nehemiah, the opposition to the rebuilding project was intense and ongoing. What Daniel prayed about in chapter 10 was most likely informed by what he saw happening with the fall and rise of empires.

Now, he was in his eighties or even maybe nineties at this point. Also, according to Daniel 1:20, he was no longer serving in an official capacity. We would say he was retired. At least he was not actively serving the king, which may explain what we read in verse 2 that he was mourning for three weeks. He couldn't do anything about the situation, so he was fasting and praying. You know what's interesting here and encouraging is Daniel was serving the Lord to the very end, and he was playing a pivotal role whether or not he had an official position. Daniel was just as effective in shaping government through his prayer to God as he was his counsel to kings. Daniel's prayer was answered by a visit and a vision that pulled back the curtain on what was happening in the spiritual realm, and it gave the assurance of what was to come over the next almost 400 years and beyond, part of which is—as we're going to talk about—a type or a shadow of what will happen in the end of time.

Let's start in Daniel 10:1–6:

> In the third year of Cyrus king of Persia a message was revealed to Daniel, whose name was called Belteshazzar. The message was true, but the appointed time was long; and he understood the message, and had understanding of the vision. In those days I, Daniel, was mourning three full weeks. I ate no pleasant food, no meat or wine came into my mouth, nor did I anoint myself at all, till three whole weeks were fulfilled.
>
> Now on the twenty-fourth day of the first month, as I was by the side of the great river, that is, the Tigris, I lifted my eyes and looked, and behold, a certain man clothed in linen, whose waist was girded with gold of Uphaz! His body was like beryl, his face like the appearance of lightning, his eyes like torches of fire, his arms and feet like burnished bronze in color, and the sound of his words like the voice of a multitude.

Now Daniel did not give us the identity. But if you look at Revelation 1:12–16, the description is very similar to the description that John gave of the exalted Jesus. Now compare the responses of the two men. Daniel said, "No strength remained in me, for my vigor was turned to frailty or ruin in me, and I retained no strength." John said it like this: "I fell at His feet as dead" (Revelation 1:17).

Look further at Daniel 10:7–11:

> And I, Daniel, alone saw the vision, for the men who were with me did not see the vision; but a great terror fell upon them, so that they fled to hide themselves. Therefore I was left alone when I saw this great vision, and no strength remained in me; for my vigor was turned to frailty in me,

> and I retained no strength. Yet I heard the sound of his words; and while I heard the sound of his words I was in a deep sleep on my face, with my face to the ground.
>
> Suddenly, a hand touched me, which made me tremble on my knees and on the palms of my hands. And he said to me, "O Daniel, man greatly beloved, understand the words that I speak to you, and stand upright, for I have now been sent to you." While he was speaking this word to me, I stood trembling.

While unnamed, we can assume that it is Gabriel, who had provided the previous interpretation of the visions.

Look at Daniel 10:12, "Then he [the man in Daniel's vision] said to me, "Do not fear, Daniel, for from the first day that you set your heart to understand, and to humble yourself before your God, your words were heard; and I have come because of your words." Now Daniel's prayer was heard from day one. But the spiritual warfare that we're going to see here in just a moment delayed the answer.

Have you ever been praying or earnestly interceding, but nothing was happening? In Luke 18, Jesus talked about how we need to be persistent in our prayers even when we're not getting an answer. Here, we are given one of the very few glimpses into the spiritual realm that is contained in the Bible. Look at Daniel 10:13–14:

> "But the prince of the kingdom of Persia withstood me twenty-one days; and behold, Michael, one of the chief princes, came to help me, for I had been left alone there with the kings of Persia. Now I have come to make you understand what will happen to your people in the latter days, for the vision refers to many days yet to come."

This is what Paul was talking about over in Ephesians 6:12, where he said, "We do not wrestle against flesh and blood, but against principalities, against powers, against the rulers of the darkness of this age, against spiritual hosts of wickedness in the heavenly places." These are the ranks of the demonic powers that are at work in the spiritual realm. We need to understand that Satan and his demons are not some type of ragtag army of darkness without a plan or a focus. Clearly, evil is marked by lawlessness, and that is their weakness, even within their own ranks. But they are not without order or structure. There are demons over territories, nations, even states, and cities, and there are those who prey upon individuals. It's very interesting to me that in recent years, as we're seeing the increase in lawlessness—which Scripture says will happen as we move toward the end times—and an increase in demonic activity, there's a lot of focus in movies about a parallel universe or multiverse. Scripture indicates that as we move toward the end of time, there will be a greater manifestation of spiritual activity.

So, what's the best way to cover it up? Well, you make it the storyline of fiction, which blurs the spiritual reality. Now, I know some may be dismissive of this idea, but look at what Paul wrote in Colossians 1:16, "For by Him all things were created that are in heaven and that are on earth, visible and invisible, whether thrones or dominions or principalities or powers. All things were created through Him and for Him." So, there's an acknowledgment in the New Testament that there is an invisible realm.

I can speak to this type of spiritual intensity that I have felt in Washington DC at various times, especially during the transfer of administrations. There's been spiritual activity. You can feel it. In fact, during 2020, as the riots were taking place across the country and in Washington DC, was a manifestation of what was happening in the spiritual realm. Again, people can be dismissive of that, but Scripture backs up that understanding.

Now, here the angel again, assuming it's Gabriel, told Daniel that he had been prevented from responding to Daniel's prayer because of the prince of Persia. Daniel was in Persia at the time. This prophecy that Daniel was about to be given covers a period, as I mentioned, of almost 400 years. But it also provides an illustration of the very end leading up to the Second Coming of Jesus Christ, again as a type.

Let's move on to Daniel 10:15, "When he had spoken such words to me, I turned my face toward the ground and became speechless." So, Daniel was told what's going to happen, and it left him speechless. Let's jump to Daniel 10:18–20:

> Then again, the one having the likeness of a man touched me and strengthened me. And he said, "O man greatly beloved, fear not! Peace be to you; be strong, yes, be strong!"
>
> So when he spoke to me I was strengthened, and said, "Let my lord speak, for you have strengthened me."
>
> Then he said, "Do you know why I have come to you? And now I must return to fight with the prince of Persia; and when I have gone forth, indeed the prince of Greece will come."

Again, the angel was battling the prince of Persia. But notice, the prince of Greece was next. That was the next world empire that would rise under Alexander the Great around 340 BC. This passage offers remarkable insight into the influence behind world leaders. There are these demonic dark princes that are the puppet masters in many ways. We've discussed this before. This is why we see history often repeating itself in various regions of the world. The demonic influences remain the same.

Let's go to Daniel 10:21, "But I will tell you what is noted in the Scripture of Truth. (No one upholds me against these, except Michael your prince)." Now this is interesting. The ESV translates that last part of v. 21: "There is none who contends by my side against these except Michael, your prince." He was referring to the angelic defense of Israel here. Specifically, the archangel Michael is the defender of the Jewish people. We also see this assertion in rabbinic tradition (e.g., Midrash Exodus Rabbah xviii.5 where it is said that Michael assisted in the Exodus and was the angelic destroyer of Sennacherib's Assyrian army). The point is that Israel has divine protection, and Michael is the agent. Otherwise, Israel has stood virtually alone as the focus and the target of global opposition, which we're going to see laid out in the next chapter.

Now, here's the application for us in this passage. And I've wrestled with this: How could the angel have delivered a vision to Daniel, a vision of what would transpire over the next almost 400 years with the amazing detail that we're going to see in the next chapter? Yet he had to battle for 21 days to get to Daniel to answer his prayer. I mean, how can the two be true? Well, here's the answer: the future is not in question. God's sovereign plan is going to be accomplished. God has a plan, and it will unfold and be fulfilled. What then *is* in question? Here's what is in question: Will our faith be strong enough for us to be a part of what God is doing?

I referred earlier to Luke 18. Let me go back to that. Luke 18:1 says, "Then He spoke a parable to them, that men always ought to pray and not lose heart." Now, in this chapter, Jesus told a parable of a widow who is relentless in trying to get justice from an unjust judge that did not want to hear her. Look at Luke 18:4–8:

> "And he [the judge] would not [grant her justice] for a while; but afterward he said within himself, 'Though I do not fear God nor regard man, yet because this widow troubles me I will avenge her, lest by her continual coming she weary me.'"
>
> Then the Lord said, "Hear what the unjust judge said. And shall God not avenge His own elect who cry out day and night to Him, though He bears long with them? I tell you that He will avenge them speedily. Nevertheless, when the Son of Man comes, will He really find faith on the earth?"

God is going to accomplish His purposes. His plan will not be frustrated by the enemy. However, the question is, where will we be as individual believers? Prayer changes us. It aligns us with what God is doing. It strengthens our faith and prepares us to join Him in what He is doing. God's plan will be accomplished. What is in question is, will we maintain our faith in Him and be a part of God's plan?

Questions for Reflection and Discussion

1. Why was the angelic messenger delayed, and how was that rectified (see vv. 12–14)?

2. What was the personal message to Daniel (see v. 19)?
   a. "Fear not."
   b. "Peace be with you."
   c. "Be strong and of good courage."
   d. All of the above

Notes on Today's Bible Reading

— Day 12 —

Today's Reading: Daniel 11

Verse of the Day

> "He shall seduce with flattery those who violate the covenant, but the people who know their God shall stand firm and take action."
>
> — *Daniel 11:32* ESV

Please read the entire Scripture selection in your own Bible and highlight or underline verses that stand out to you before you read the observations and engage the questions below.

Daniel 11 is another chapter where critics try to claim that the book of Daniel could not have been written by Daniel in the time period commonly claimed because the prophecy is too accurate. There's too much detail to have been predicted hundreds of years beforehand. Well, that's not surprising. These are the same sort of individuals who question the sovereignty of God.

What we read here is an amazing chapter of biblical prophecy that was given to Daniel, which will cover a period of almost five centuries. In the time after Daniel and those who followed—which includes Ezra, Nehemiah, Haggai, Zechariah, and Malachi—there was a period of about 400 years in which there were no active prophets. There was no word from God to His people. This is called the Intertestamental Period. It's the 400 years between the Old Testament and the New Testament. Some would say, "Well, why did God not speak?" We don't know for certain. Some suggest it was because the people of God were not listening. Regardless, what we do know is that this word given to Daniel and other prophets covers this period so that the people were not left without a word from God. Therefore, they were not without hope during a very difficult and dark period in the history of their nation.

Let's begin in Daniel 11:1, "Also in the first year of Darius the Mede, I, even I, stood up to confirm and strengthen him." Now, this is a continuation from chapter 10, where the angel that we believe to be Gabriel said that he was involved in the strengthening of Darius, who could refer to Astyages, the last king of the Medes. But "Darius" simply means "Lord." Consequently, some scholars believe that's a title, not a proper name, and it's a reference to Cyrus and his decision to allow the Jews to return to Jerusalem. This episode again provides insight into the spiritual battle that's taking place, and it shows very clearly why we need to be praying for government, as we're instructed.

Let's continue in Daniel 11:2, "And now I will tell you the truth: Behold, three more kings will arise in Persia, and the fourth shall be far richer than them all; by his strength, through his riches, he shall stir up all against the realm of Greece." Now this prophecy is referring to Xerxes, the final king in Persia. He went to war against the Greeks, and he failed. Then we see this in Daniel 11:3–4:

> "Then a mighty king shall arise, who shall rule with great dominion, and do according to his will. And when he has arisen, his kingdom shall be broken up and divided toward

> the four winds of heaven, but not among his posterity nor according to his dominion with which he ruled; for his kingdom shall be uprooted, even for others besides these."

The subject matter of this final vision is the same that we saw in the dream of Nebuchadnezzar in chapter 2 and Daniel's vision in chapters 7 and 8: the four world kingdoms and where they are ultimately leading. With each successive dream or vision, what we see is a focus on the subsequent kingdom. So here the focus is on the two great kingdoms that arise out of the remains of Alexander the Great. I encourage you to look into the historical record because it's amazing when you look at this prophecy and compare it to history. This prophecy has been fulfilled, and frankly it's quite remarkable.

Now, Alexander's empire was divided among his four generals, but for the purposes our Bible study we will only focus on two of those generals. Ptolemy in the south ruled over Egypt, Arabia, Libya, Ethiopia, and some of the other countries. Lucius to the north ruled over Syria, and that became a kingdom. Now, the two battled back and forth. And guess who was in the middle as we read here in v 16? Right, we are told the "glorious land" of Israel. Now Israel got bounced back and forth, alternately being dominated by the North or the South, and this went on for about 150 years. Then we get to the "little horn" from the North in this passage, which was first spoken of over in Daniel 8:9. This ruler is an enemy of God, a persecutor of God's people: Antiochus IV, who liked to be called "Epiphanes," which means "God manifest" because he believed himself to be the incarnation of the Greek god Zeus.

Let's pick up in Daniel 11:21, which gives us more on this arrogant and evil individual, "And in his place shall arise a vile person, to whom they will not give the honor of royalty; but he shall come in peaceably, and seize the kingdom by intrigue." Throughout history we see these patterns which we've discussed. History repeats itself, and there's a reason. It's due to the forces behind it. But here we also have a type and a foreshadowing of the Antichrist. So, we should closely observe his characteristics: He is pompous, he is vile, and he gains power peaceably by intrigue, by flattery, and by deception. I won't go into all the history of Antiochus, but you can see that this prophecy is borne out in the historical record.

Let's continue in Daniel 11:22–27:

> "With the force of a flood they shall be swept away from before him and be broken, and also the prince of the covenant. And after the league is made with him he shall act deceitfully, for he shall come up and become strong with a small number of people. He shall enter peaceably, even into the richest places of the province; and he shall do what his fathers have not done, nor his forefathers: he shall disperse among them the plunder, spoil, and riches; and he shall devise his plans against the strongholds, but only for a time.
>
> "He shall stir up his power and his courage against the king of the South with a great army. And the king of the South shall be stirred up to battle with a very great and mighty army; but he shall not stand, for they shall devise plans against him. Yes, those who eat of the portion of his delicacies shall destroy him; his army shall be swept away, and many shall fall down slain. Both these kings' hearts shall be bent on evil, and they shall speak lies at the same table; but it shall not prosper, for the end will still be at the appointed time."

So again, this is prophecy being fulfilled in history, but it's also a type. There was an agreement between the North and the South, but they did not speak truth. This is often the case. We've seen this even in relatively modern history. We saw this in the agreement between the three allied countries coming out of World War II, Russia, Great Britain, and America. There was great deception from Russia. They took over Eastern Europe, ruling with a strong Communist hand for nearly 50 years. So, we look at these patterns that are a precursor to the end-times.

Let's drop down to Daniel 11:31–32:

> "And forces shall be mustered by him, and they shall defile the sanctuary fortress; then they shall take away the daily sacrifices, and place there the abomination of desolation. Those who do wickedly against the covenant he shall corrupt with flattery; but the people who know their God shall be strong, and carry out great exploits."

The Jewish people were no threat to Antiochus, but he hated the Jewish people. The identification with God and the blessing of God upon a people often incites the enemies of God against those people.

History confirms that during the time of Antiochus some of the Jewish leaders aligned with him and aided him. The book of Maccabees (which is not in the canon of Scripture because of some of the aspects of the theological assertions there are in conflict with the rest of Scripture) provides a historical account of this period of time. It records that Jason, the brother of the Jewish high priest, aided Antiochus in his deception and his coming into Jerusalem.

The book also records the actions of the Maccabees who stood firm, took action against Antiochus, and defeated him and his armies after Antiochus defiled the temple. Now this was a horrific time for the Jewish people. Thousands were killed and slaughtered by Antiochus, who was pure evil.

Look at Daniel 11:33–35:

> "And those of the people who understand shall instruct many; yet for many days they shall fall by sword and flame, by captivity and plundering. Now when they fall, they shall be aided with a little help; but many shall join with them by intrigue. And some of those of understanding shall fall, to refine them, purify them, and make them white, until the time of the end; because it is still for the appointed time."

Again, we've seen these patterns play out in history, not just in this period, but even in modern history, in 1930s and 1940s during the Holocaust directed by Hitler. While the rest of the chapter continues the narrative of Antiochus and what he did, there is a shift in focus to the future, with a greater focus on the Antichrist and the end times, according to many scholars.

This focus shift begins in Daniel 11:36, "Then the king shall do according to his own will: he shall exalt and magnify himself above every god, shall speak blasphemies against the God of gods, and shall prosper till the wrath has been accomplished; for what has been determined shall be done." Now we know from Revelation that the Antichrist will be able to wreak havoc on the world for a set period of time. He will use religion to exalt himself and to be worshipped as a God. Look at Daniel 11:37–38:

> "He shall regard neither the God of his fathers nor the desire of women, nor regard any god; for he shall exalt himself above them all. But in their place he shall honor a god of fortresses; and a god which his fathers did not know he shall honor with gold and silver, with precious stones and pleasant things."

There will be a lot of deception in the end times. When Jesus' disciples asked Him about when the end would come, His reply in Mark 13 was "Take heed that no one deceives you." The antidote to deception is truth, that is why knowing and yielding to the word of God is so important.

Look at Daniel 11:39, "Thus he shall act against the strongest fortresses with a foreign god, which he shall acknowledge, and advance its glory; and he shall cause them to rule over many, and divide the land for gain." Drop down to the last verse of this chapter, Daniel 11:45, "And he shall plant the tents of his palace between the seas and the glorious holy mountain; yet he shall come to his end, and no one will help him." Again, Antiochus is a type of Antichrist. This is the pattern we've seen before in history. And of course we ask the question "When will the final fulfillment of this prophecy come?" We don't know.

But here's what I want you to take away from this chapter: This prophecy was designed to encourage God's people that there was a light at the end of the tunnel during a very dark and difficult time. God was assuring them that His plan and purposes would be accomplished. The same is true for where we stand today. Knowing that the history of the world has been written, and we have it in Scripture, we know how it will unfold. Now, it's kind of like a coloring book. The prophetic lines are drawn, but the fulfillment in history is going to be colored in between now and the end. But we know where it's leading, and we can take great comfort in that. And just as Daniel prayed, we need to be praying as the warfare around us is raging. Praying for the plans and purposes of God promised in His word would come to pass. I would add that our prayers should be supercharged by the fulfillment of God's word right before our eyes.

Again, this is an amazing passage of Scripture. I encourage you to read the whole thing. It would be helpful, obviously, to have some of the solid older commentaries, which you can find online. Matthew Henry wrote a good commentary on Daniel, and there are others that help fill in some of the spaces. But I do encourage you to read the book of Daniel and pray through it as you read it and be encouraged by it.

Questions for Reflection and Discussion

1. Who is the ruthless ruler who comes against God's people in the "glorious land" of Israel in Daniel's more immediate future (see 11:21–35)?
   a. Xerxes
   b. Alexander the Great
   c. Antiochus IV Epiphanes
   d. None of the above

2. Who is the deceptive and dominant end-times ruler described in 11:36–45?

Notes on Today's Bible Reading

— Day 13 —

Today's Reading: Daniel 12

Verse of the Day

> "He said, 'Go your way, Daniel, for the words are closed up and sealed till the time of the end.'"
>
> — *Daniel 12:9*

Please read the entire Scripture selection in your own Bible and highlight or underline verses that stand out to you before you read the observations and engage the questions below.

Today, we finish the last recorded vision of Daniel as we complete the book of Daniel with chapter 12. Our key verse is Daniel 12:9, which says, "And he said, 'Go your way, Daniel, for the words are closed up and sealed till the time of the end.'" As I've said before: I am not an expert on biblical prophecy. I'm sharing with you my understanding, and frankly, just as Daniel said: his understanding was limited, so is mine. He asked for greater understanding, and I've done the same. And I encourage you to do the same because we've seen even in this passage where this prophecy was sealed, meaning that the complete understanding was held back. Yet I do believe we live in an age when God is opening the Scripture to us through the Holy Spirit. In fact, in Revelation 22:10, John was told the very opposite of what Daniel was told. Revelation 22:10 says, "[The angel] said to me, '*Do not seal* the words of the prophecy of this book, for the time is at hand'" (italics added). I would say that is for those who have ears to hear the Word of God is speaking because I believe we are in that time of revelation.

Chapter 12 predicts two great periods of distress in the future presented in such a way that they appear to be one. Yet the prophecy applies to both. In the near term, this vision describes the time of Antiochus, as we saw in chapter 10. It was a horrific period of time for the Jewish people, but it also applies to the time of the Antichrist, which is yet to come. Let's start in Daniel 12:1–2:

> "At that time Michael shall stand up,
> The great prince who stands watch over the sons of your people;
> And there shall be a time of trouble,
> Such as never was since there was a nation,
> Even to that time.
> And at that time your people shall be delivered,
> Every one who is found written in the book.
> And many of those who sleep in the dust of the earth shall
> awake,
> Some to everlasting life,
> Some to shame and everlasting contempt."

These opening verses are clearly looking beyond Antiochus's time to that of the end of the Great Tribulation period. Some students of the Bible believe that at the return of Jesus after the rapture of the church and the tribulation period has been completed, the Old Testament saints will be resurrected and be a part of the millennial reign of Christ. Now in verse 2, it reads that the righteous and the unrighteous are resurrected. That will occur, but not necessarily at the same time. Revelation 20 speaks of another resurrection at the end of the thousand-year period when the Great White Throne judgment occurs (see vv. 5, 11–15).

Let's continue in Daniel 12:3–4:

> "Those who are wise shall shine
> Like the brightness of the firmament,
> And those who turn many to righteousness
> Like the stars forever and ever.
>
> "But you, Daniel, shut up the words, and seal the book until the time of the end; many shall run to and fro, and knowledge shall increase."

There is a lot of debate over what verse 4 is saying. Some interpret this to mean people near the end of time will be searching for the answers, and they'll read the prophecies of Daniel and others and will gain knowledge. I think this is a very plausible interpretation. Others see this as a prophetic description of the final days of people literally going from one place to another, back and forth.

As I edit this final chapter, I am sitting in the De Gaulle Airport in Paris waiting for my flight to Tel Aviv. We live in an unparalleled age of global transportation. Knowledge shall increase. Now we live in what is called the Information Age. According to experts who study this, information is expanding ten times faster than the growth of any other manufactured or natural product. According to their studies, information has been increasing at a rate of 66% per year for many decades. Artificial Intelligence (AI) is going to accelerate it even more. Now, just a footnote to that: Information and knowledge have expanded greatly, but not wisdom, which is the rightful application of knowledge and information. I would argue that wisdom is actually decreasing.

Let's continue in Daniel 12:5–8:

> Then I, Daniel, looked; and there stood two others, one on this riverbank and the other on that riverbank. And one said to the man clothed in linen, who was above the waters of the river, "How long shall the fulfillment of these wonders be?"
>
> Then I heard the man clothed in linen, who was above the waters of the river, when he held up his right hand and his left hand to heaven, and swore by Him who lives forever, that it shall be for a time, times, and half a time; and when the power of the holy people has been completely shattered, all these things shall be finished.
>
> Although I heard, I did not understand. Then I said, "My lord, what shall be the end of these things?"

Again Daniel, who was given this prophetic message, was asking for an understanding of where this was headed and when it would take place. Daniel 12:9 says, "And He [the man clothed in linen] said, 'Go your way, Daniel, for the words are closed up and sealed till the time of the end.'" Not everything is told to him. Obviously, in Revelation, John was given more, and I think the two go together. Look at Daniel 12:10, "Many shall be purified, made white, and refined, but the wicked shall do wickedly; and none of the wicked shall understand, but the wise shall understand." There is a reason we are given just enough information to know that something is coming, that it's going to happen, but not exactly what, when and how.

Again, this dovetails perfectly with the New Testament and what Jesus had to say over in Luke 12:35–39:

> "Let your waist be girded and your lamps burning; and you yourselves be like men who wait for their master, when he will return from the wedding, that when he comes and knocks they may open to him immediately. Blessed are those servants whom the master, when he comes, will find watching. Assuredly, I say to you that he will gird himself and have them sit down to eat, and will come and serve them. And if he should come in the second watch, or come in the third watch, and find them so, blessed are those servants. But know this, that if the master of the house had known what hour the thief would come, he would have watched and not allowed his house to be broken into."

We should live with expectation of the return of Jesus, so that we are found faithful. The remaining verses of Daniel 12 speak to the abomination. This is the profaning of the temple by Antiochus in 145 BC when he sacrificed a pig in the temple. Again, this action was a type of the great abomination that will ultimately be fulfilled by the Antichrist in the Great Tribulation period.

Unfortunately, time does not allow me to delve into the numbers in any depth. I have seen many different calculations of the numbers that we read in these following verses. The numbers have both a symbolic and a literal meaning, as seven is the number of completion and three and a half is partial completion. These days, as we know, can also be calculated as years. Look at Daniel 12:11, "And from the time that the daily sacrifice is taken away, and the abomination of desolation is set up, there shall be one thousand two hundred and ninety days."

Now this is a month beyond the times and half, which is three and a half years, which was made reference to above. Then we see yet another period of time. Look at Daniel 12:12, "Blessed is he who waits, and comes to the one thousand three hundred and thirty-five days." Again, there are a lot of different interpretations for these, both in days in terms of the tribulation period and years leading up to that, because this is another 45 days added to that. You can read some of the commentaries for differing views as to how to apply those numbers.

Let's continue with Daniel 12:13, "But you, go your way till the end; for you shall rest, and will arise to your inheritance at the end of the days." I believe God was saying: "I'm giving you this word: You're going to die, but you're going to be resurrected again to be a part of this in the end days." Fascinating. And again, prophecy is here for us to learn from so we can live with anticipation and expectation of the return of Christ.

Finally, let's wrap up our study of this chapter and the book of Daniel with three takeaways or action steps:

1. Secure Your Destination

The sequence and specifics of end-time events should not be our main pursuit. The more important pursuit is whether your name is "written in the book" (Daniel 12:1). Life's biggest decision is whether you choose Christ and follow Him above everyone and everything else. Jesus made that same point to the disciples after their triumphant return from casting out demons in Luke 10:20, He told them to rejoice over the fact that their names are written in heaven. John repeatedly referred to the "Book of Life" in Revelation (3:5; 17:8; 20:12, 15), finally calling it "the Lamb's Book of Life" (21:27). Is your name written there? First, secure your place in the book.

2. Shine in the Darkness

We see that in Daniel 12:3 and 10. Verse 10 says: "Many shall be purified, made spotless and refined." So we're to pursue righteousness, knowing that ultimately, we are clothed with the righteousness of Christ, but we're also to "turn many to righteousness" (v. 3). Joining God on His rescue mission to seek and save the lost is far more important than speculating on the minute details of future events. In fact, when the angel told Daniel to "go your way," it reminds me of how Jesus put it in the Great Commission. The Greek literally says: "as you go make disciples" (see Matt. 28:19). Pursuing righteousness and turning others to righteousness, will cause us to shine like stars against the blackness of the night that will mark the end times. So secure your destination, your place in "the Book," shine in the darkness, and finally…

3. Stand in Your Designated Place

The NKJV renders the final verse of the book: "But you, go your way till the end; for you shall rest, and will arise to your inheritance at the end of the days." Interestingly, the ESV renders Daniel 12:13b this way: "And you shall rest and shall stand in your allotted place at the end of the days."

The Hebrew word translated "allotted" is the same one used for the land allotments each tribe was designated in the book of Joshua. This speaks of the reward that is promised for all believers.

A share in the rule of the nations is ours under the overall reign of King Jesus during Messiah's earthly millennial kingdom. For that we wait with great anticipation.

Yet I couldn't help but notice that Daniel was told that, after his "rest" or death, he would "stand." When the trumpet sounds, Jesus descends, and the dead are raised, Daniel and all saints will stand on a renewed earth. We will stand in the place designated to us, allotted to us as our reward. What a day that will be!

In light of that day, how should it motivate us to live now? We must stand! In fact, the Hebrew word translated "stand" here means "to take one's stand," "to be in a standing attitude," "to be steadfast," "to make a stand and hold one's ground." In light of this verse, may I give you one final challenge from Daniel? Until that day when you are laid to rest, stand in the place God has designated for you to serve Him. See, it all comes back to Ephesians 6:13 and the call to armor up and take our stand. Then once we have prayed, prepared, and taken our stand, then by all means, keep on standing!

Questions for Reflection and Discussion

1. What end-time events are referred to in Daniel 12:1–2?
   a. Great Tribulation
   b. Deliverance of a remnant of Israel
   c. Resurrection of the just and unjust
   d. All of the above

2. What actions are those who are "wise" to take until the end (see v. 3)?

Notes on Today's Bible Reading

Appendix 1:
Stand on the Word Bible Reading Plan

Visit frc.org/Bible for our chronological journey through the Bible that we call "Stand on the Word." We encourage you to spend time reading and studying the Bible because it is literally "God-breathed" (2 Timothy 3:16 NIV); it is God's very words to us. The Bible answers the big questions, such as *Why am I here? Where did I come from? Where am I going (life after death)? If God is good, why does evil and suffering exist?* The Bible not only answers these big questions; it offers practical advice in areas such as *How can I deal with feelings of fear or anger or guilt? How can I forgive when I cannot forget? What should I look for in a spouse? How can I have a successful marriage? How can I be a good parent? What is my spiritual gift and place in the church? What is my stewardship responsibility as a citizen?* We learned the verse in Bible school, "Your word is a lamp to my feet / And a light to my path" (Psalm 119:105). God's Word shows us the way forward in any area of life and on every question we face.

The Stand on the Word Bible Reading Plan takes us through the Bible chronologically. In other words, each reading takes you through the Bible as events occurred in history as far as it is possible. Here is how it works for our family. At the same time each morning, whether I am at home, in Washington, or in some foreign country, I send my wife and children a morning greeting along with a reminder of the passage for the day. The text includes two questions related to the reading. The questions are designed to help with content retention, to serve as an accountability tool, and to provide for discussion.

The two-year plan does not have a Sunday passage. Instead, it provides an outline for a family discussion that can be done on Sunday afternoon or evening each week. The weekly discussion time begins with a spiritual leader asking each person individually for one or two insights or truths they gained from their reading during the week. After everyone else shares, you can then lead a short discussion based upon one of the passages that you read in the week just completed. It is also a time for them to ask questions.

By the way, you don't have to have all the answers. If you don't know, tell them so and then talk to your pastor or other trusted person with Bible knowledge. If your children start asking questions, that suggests they are thinking about what they are reading.

Reading God's Word will help you establish a fruitful walk with the God who made you and loves you. Whether you are single or married, this plan will enable you to lead your friends and family in reading God's Word daily. The added benefit is that you will all be reading the same text together. It will amaze you to see how God speaks sometimes in the same ways and at other times in different ways to each of you. Being on this journey together will build a spiritual synergy, a deep bond, and sense of unity and purpose like nothing else! Use it to impart the Word of life.

Appendix 2:
Prayer: Talking with God

Most Americans say they pray. But not as many pray the way Jesus did and the way He taught His disciples to pray. Fewer, still, really know the power in prayer that God gave us to impact our families, communities, nation, and world. But prayer is our lifeline to God, our means of communicating with our Heavenly Father. It develops our relationship—our friendship, fellowship, and intimacy—with Him. In prayer we experience God and are "filled with the Spirit" (Ephesians 5:18). God uses the prayers of faithful men, women, boys, and girls to heal broken lives and strengthen families, churches, communities, and even nations. He uses our prayers to advance His Kingdom on earth (Daniel 9; Acts 4:36)! He wants to use all believers!

The Essence of Prayer

Prayer is simply talking with God—about anything and everything. He is our Maker, Father, Savior, Provider, and Counselor; our Master, Healer, Guide, and Friend. Christ died for our sins and rose from the dead to sit at the right hand of God the Father, where He is praying for us right now (Hebrews 10:12; 7:25). His Spirit now lives within us and helps us to pray (Romans 8:9, 26).

The Priority of Prayer

Jesus spent time alone with God regularly, drawing strength from the Father and seeking His will for every decision (Luke 6:12–13; 22:39–44). His disciples asked Jesus to teach them how to pray (Luke 11:1–13). The apostles knew that prayer and obedience were the keys to Christ's life and ministry and were determined to follow His example: "We will devote ourselves to prayer and to the ministry of the word" (Acts 6:4 ESV). Yet too few American men pray today, even pastors and leaders! Yet strong praying men are the norm in Scripture. Our families, churches, and nation need men who will make prayer a priority today (1 Timothy 2:8).

The Practice of Prayer

Scripture teaches, "Pray continually!" (1 Thessalonians 5:17 NIV); "praying always" (Ephesians 6:18); "always pray and [do] not give up" (Luke 18:1 NIV). Below are some helps to get you started. No one can beat the Lord's Prayer. It is an outline of key themes to guide our prayer lives:

"Our Father in heaven,
hallowed be your name.
Your kingdom come,
your will be done,
    on earth as it is in heaven.
Give us this day our daily bread,
and forgive us our debts,
    as we also have forgiven our debtors.

And lead us not into temptation,
but deliver us from evil." (Matthew 6:9–13)

In the book of Psalms and throughout Scripture, God has sprinkled prayers: patterns for us to learn from. Here is a simple, popular acronym to help jog our memories:

P-R-A-Y:

- *Praise:* Our Father which art in heaven, hallowed be Thy name.
- *Repent:* And forgive us our debts, as we forgive our debtors.
- *Ask:* Give us this day our daily bread. And forgive us our debts, as we forgive our debtors. And lead us not into temptation but deliver us from evil.
- *Yield:* Thy kingdom come. Thy will be done in earth, as it is in heaven.

Praying through Scripture

God also talks to us. The Bible is His Word (2 Timothy 2:15; 3:16). Bible in hand, we should pray God's promises back to Him and claim them for our families, our work, our finances, and our nation (1 Timothy 2:1–8; 1 John 5:14–15).

Scriptures to Pray as a Man: Joshua 1:8; 1 Timothy 3:1–15; 1 Chronicles 12:32; 1 Timothy 6:1–12; 1 Corinthians 16:13; Romans 12:1–21; Micah 6:8; John 4:24; Acts 2:38: 1 Kings 2:2; Husbands: Ephesians 5:25–28; Genesis 2:24; 1 Peter 3:7; Ephesians 4:26–27; Matthew 5:32; Proverbs 5:19; 1 Corinthians 6:18; Fathers: Deuteronomy 4:8–10; 11:18–21; Exodus 34:5–8; Psalm 127:3–5; Matthew 7:11; Ephesians 6:4; Proverbs 22:6; Luke 11:11–12; Hebrews 12:5–7

Scriptures to Pray as a Woman: Matthew 22:36–40; Proverbs 31:30; 1 Peter 3:1–3; Ephesians 5:26; Ephesians 4:15, 29; 1 Timothy 3:11; Ephesians 5:22, 24; 1 Peter 3:1–2; Philippians 4:10– 13; Philippians 2:3–4; Proverbs 31:12; 1 Corinthians 7:34; Titus 2:3–4; Titus 2:4–5; James 1:19; Ephesians 4:32; 1 Corinthians 7:1–5; Luke 2:37; Colossians 4:2; Proverbs 31:27; 1 Timothy 5:14; 1 Timothy 5:14

Scriptures to Pray for Your Children: Matthew 22:36–40; 2 Timothy 3:15; Psalm 97:10, 38:18; Proverbs 8:13; John 17:15, 10:10; Romans 12:9; Psalm 119:71; Hebrews 12:5–6; Daniel 1:17, 20; Proverbs 1:4; James 1:5; Romans 13:1; Ephesians 6:1–3; Hebrews 13:17; Proverbs 1:10–16; 13:20; 2 Corinthians 6:14–17; Deuteronomy 6; 1 Corinthians 6:18–20; Acts 24:16; 1 Timothy 1:19, 4:1–2; Titus 1:15–16; Psalm 23:4; Deuteronomy 10:12; Matthew 28:18–20; Ephesians 1:3, 4:29; Ephesians 1:16–19; Philippians 1:11; Colossians 1:9; Philippians 1:9–10

Developing Personal Prayer Habits

Rise early each day to pray with opened Bible. Daniel prayed three times daily. Pray whenever you can: as you drive, with your spouse, with your children at dinner, on the phone with a friend, and before bedtime. You cannot pray too much!

Praying Together with Others

Pray with your spouse regularly. Make time for family prayer. Be part of your church prayer meeting or group. Christ said, "My house shall be called a house of prayer" (Matthew 21:13; Mark 11:17; Luke 19:46). The apostle Paul instructed Pastor Timothy (1 Timothy 2:1–8) to make prayer the first order of the church, saying prayer is key to peace in the nation. There is nothing like a

Spirit-led prayer meeting with people who love the Lord! Praying women have been standing in the prayer gap for decades. Every man must set his heart to become a praying man, lead his family in prayer, and be a strong contributor to the corporate prayer life of his church. We must be leaders in praying for our morally and spiritually troubled, divided nation—and for our national leaders. American Christians simply must respond to God's promise in 2 Chronicles 7:14:

> "If My people who are called by My name will humble themselves, and pray and seek My face, and turn from their wicked ways, then I will hear from heaven, and will forgive their sin and will their land."

Prayer As Warfare

Jesus described the enemy, the devil, as a thief whose mission is to "steal, and to kill, and to destroy" (John 10:10). Demonic forces are at war against everything good in you, your family, your church, your community, America, and every nation (Ephesians 6:10–20).

The devil and his minions are out to thwart the Kingdom of God and eliminate righteousness wherever he can. He hates God, hates people and will use spiritually ignorant and deceived men, women, boys, and girls to do his bidding. Men of God today, like the sons of Issachar in ancient Israel, need to understand the times and know what the church and our nation must do (1 Chronicles 12:32). We must pull down Satan's strongholds, wrestle for our families, and use Spirit-led prayer and wisdom to help guide our churches and communities to prevail against the evil onslaught against us (2 Corinthians 10:3–5). This is the war of the ages, and it is real.

Finally, Determine to Become a Person of Prayer

No matter how long you have been a Christian and may have neglected prayer up until now, you can become a person of prayer starting today. If you have missed the mark, it is not too late. Call upon the Lord, ask His help, and proceed with His guidance.

O Lord, make me a praying person; make me a prayer warrior! In Jesus' name, amen!

Book Study Discipleship Tool:
To Help You Use This Book in Small Groups

Agenda

Getting Acquainted

You only get one chance to start. So, having everyone there to meet everyone, learn names, and connect on a "level playing field" is crucial. Do not be so structured in following this conversation guide you keep the Holy Spirit from moving in your group. This is intended to show you one way to navigate your time together.

Conversation Guide

The most important thing you're going to do as you start your group is *listen*. The leader who is doing all the talking is not a great small-group leader.

1. What happened last week you are thankful for?
    - Everyone needs to answer briefly.
2. What challenge is happening in your life, family, or community?
    - Everyone needs to answer briefly.
    - Ask for a volunteer to pray for each person by name.
    - Pray for everyone by name

- Thank God for all the blessings on our lives
- Pray for the challenges we are facing.

3. Ask if everyone was able to read the assigned chapter.
4. Ask everyone to share one main takeaway from the chapter.
5. Work through the discussion questions in the back of the chapter.
6. Once everyone has had a chance to answer the questions at the end of the chapter, ask the following questions:
   - Ask, "From what you have read this week and what we discussed today/tonight, what is your 'I will' statement? How are you going to apply this lesson/truth?"
   - Assign the next reading assignment/chapter for the group and confirm date and time of next meeting
   - Ask, "Does anyone feel led to close in prayer?" If no one volunteers, the group leader will voice a short prayer and close out the group.

Outline and Tips

Books

The first order of business is your book order. Be sure to order your books one month in advance from your first group meeting. It is critical that everyone leave your group on Launch Night with the book in hand.

When you realize the average American reads 2.4 books per year, you begin to grasp the potential impact reading one solid Christian book can have on a person. And reading books in a high accountability context is more like graduate school than reading in a recliner. Knowing you're going to be held accountable for learning the key takeaways and having a conversation with your group about the book will make the learning experience really rich. The best group leaders share from their own well of knowledge and experience, so using a book that really speaks to you is best.

Calendar

One of the most "mission critical" activities you'll do at your first session will be setting the calendar for the season. You and your group will need to decide how often you will meet as a group (weekly or biweekly) and how long you will meet. Set targets for when you will begin and end. This will prevent the meeting from taking too long.

Location & Group Size

Keep the groups small. (Ideally four to six.) Divide larger groups into subgroups and have them work through the questions simultaneously. Plan in advance the location and environment for your group. Make sure you'll have a comfortable place for everyone. Whether around a dining room table, in a den, or at another location, be sure your location is conducive to conversation and prayer. All this will help draw quiet or shy people into the discussion.

Friendship & Transparency

Another important thing is friendship. You're going to need to be a *friend* to your group members. Invest in them by loving them unconditionally: this means loving them where they are, showing them you're their friend, and listening to them intently. *Transparency* is another important part of being a group leader. This book you will read together is important and the prayer time is critical, but the real impact of a mature group leader is in sharing his life experiences, both good and bad. This is invaluable.

Prayer

Praying for your group and leading your group to pray for each other is huge. Be intentional about this orienting your group to God, encouraging your group to pray for each other and for you between sessions.*

*Adapted from Final Command Ministries Discovery Group Questions. Used by permission.

Notes

1. https://georgebarna.com/product/raising-spiritual-champions-book/.

2. Philip Schaff, *History of the Christian Church*, 8 vols. (New York: Charles Scribner's Sons, 1910), 7:245.

3. Henry H. Halley, *Halley's Bible Handbook: Classic Edition* (Grand Rapids, MI: Zondervan, 2000), 440.

4. Ibid.

5. Ibid.

6. Ibid., 441.

Other Study Guides Available from
Fidelis Publishing and Family Research Council

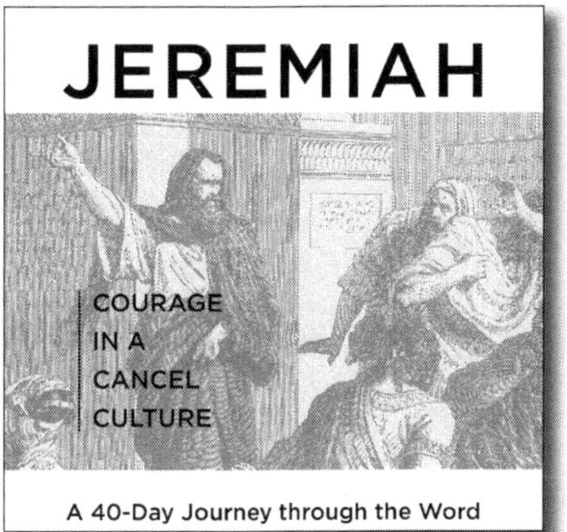

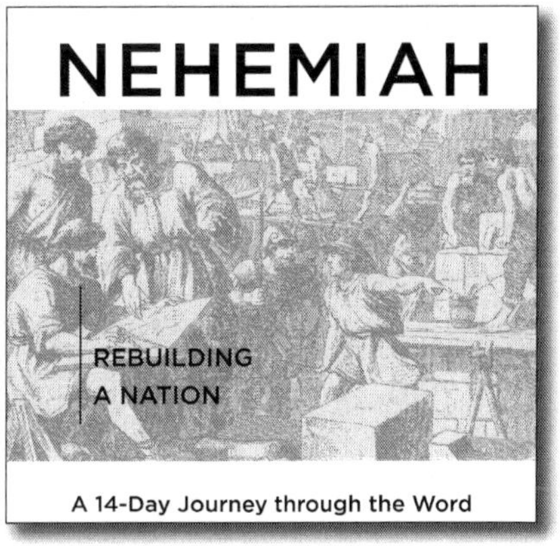

STAND on the WORD

Jeremiah: Courage in a Cancel Culture ISBN: 9781956454369

Nehemiah: Rebuilding a Nation ISBN: 9781956454468

Ephesians: Keep Standing! ISBN: 9781956454659

Joshua: Finish Strong! ISBN: 9781956454802

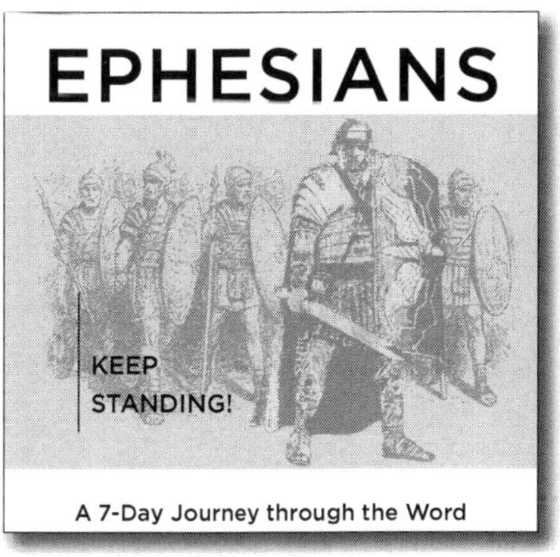

Also from Fidelis Publishing and Family Research Council

STAND on the WORD Journals

Volume 1
ISBN: 9781956454758

Volume 2
ISBN: 9781956454871